Fashion, Costume, and Culture

Clothing, Headwear, Body Decorations, and Footwear Through the Ages

SECOND EDITION

Fashion, Costume, and Culture

Clothing, Headwear, Body Decorations, and Footwear Through the Ages

VOLUME 4

MODERN WORLD PART I: 1900 TO 1945

SECOND EDITION

Sara Pendergast, Tom Pendergast, and Drew D. Johnson, Editors
Julie L. Carnagie, Project Editor

U·X·L
A part of Gale, Cengage Learning

Detroit • New York • San Francisco • New Haven, Conn • Waterville, Maine • London

GALE
CENGAGE Learning·

Fashion, Costume, and Culture:
Clothing, Headwear, Body
Decorations, and Footwear
Through the Ages, 2nd ed.

Sara Pendergast, Tom Pendergast,
and Drew D. Johnson, Editors

Project Editor: Julie L. Carnagie

Editorial: Sarah Hermsen

Rights Acquisition and Management: Christine Myaskovsky

Composition: Evi Abou-El-Seoud

Manufacturing: Wendy Blurton

Imaging: John Watkins

Product Design: Kristine Julien

For product information and technology assistance, contact us at
Gale Customer Support, 1-800-877-4253.
For permission to use material from this text or product, submit all requests
online at **www.cengage.com/permissions**.
Further permissions questions can be emailed to
permissionrequest@cengage.com

Cover photos reproduced by permission of: Volume 1 (from left to right), ©PRISMA ARCHIVO/
Alamy; ©Mariano Garcia/Alamy; ©J Marshall - Tribaleye Images/Alamy; ©Ive Close Images/
Alamy;. Volume 2 (from left to right), ©Bachmann/F1online digitale Bildagentur GmbH/
Alamy; ©Gavin Hellier/Jon Arnold Images Ltd/Alamy ©Pete Saloutos/Corbis Bridge/Alamy;
© North Wind Picture Archives/Alamy. Volume 3 (from left to right), ©Amoret Tanner/Alamy;
©Thislife Then/thislife pictures/Alamy; ©Classic Image/Alamy; © Walker Art Library/Alamy.
Volume 4 (from left to right), ©H. ARMSTRONG ROBERTS/ClassicStock/Alamy; ©Thislife Then/
thislife pictures/Alamy; H. ARMSTRONG ROBERTS/ClassicStock/Alamy; ©Amoret Tanner/Alamy.
Volume 5 (from left to right), ©Michael Ayre/Alamy; © Duncan Davis/Alamy; ©H. ARMSTRONG
ROBERTS/ClassicStock/Alamy; ©H. ARMSTRONG ROBERTS/ClassicStock/Alamy. Volume 6 (from
left to right), ©Robert Slade/Manor Photography/Alamy; ©Craig Eisenberg/Alamy; ©Richard
Newton/Alamy; © Ingram Publishing/Alamy.

While every effort has been made to ensure the reliability of the information presented in this
publication, Gale, a part of Cengage Learning, does not guarantee the accuracy of the data
contained herein. Gale accepts no payment for listing; and inclusion in the publication of any
organization, agency, institution, publication, service, or individual does not imply endorsement
of the editors or publisher. Errors brought to the attention of the publisher and verified to the
satisfaction of the publisher will be corrected in future editions.

LIBRARY OF CONGRESS CATALOGING-IN-PUBLICATION DATA

Fashion, costume, and culture: clothing, headwear, body decorations, and
    footwear through the ages Drew D. Johnson, Julie L. Carnagie,
    editors. — 2nd ed.
    6 v. p. cm.
    Includes bibliographical references and index.
    ISBN 978-1-4144-9841-6 (set : alk. paper) — ISBN 978-1-4144-9842-3 (vol. 1 :
alk. paper) — ISBN 978-1-4144-9843-0 (vol. 2 : alk. paper) — ISBN 978-1-4144-
9844-7 (vol. 3 : alk. paper) — ISBN 978-1-4144-9845-4 (vol. 4 : alk. paper) —
ISBN 978-1-4144-9846-1 (vol. 5 : alk. paper) — ISBN 978-1-4144-9847-8 (vol. 6 :
alk. paper)

1. Clothing and dress—History. 2. Fashion—History. 3. Body marking—History.
4. Dress accessories—History. I. Johnson, Drew D. II. Carnagie, Julie L.

GT511.F358 2013
391—dc232012026648

Gale
27500 Drake
Farmington Hills, MI, 48331-3535

978-1-4144-9841-6 (set)   1-4144-9841-1 (set)
978-1-4144-9842-3 (vol. 1)   1-4144-9842-X (vol. 1)
978-1-4144-9843-0 (vol. 2)   1-4144-9843-8 (vol. 2)
978-1-4144-9844-7 (vol. 3)   1-4144-9844-6 (vol. 3)
978-1-4144-9845-4 (vol. 4)   1-4144-9845-4 (vol. 4)
978-1-4144-9846-1 (vol. 5)   1-4144-9846-2 (vol. 5)
978-1-4144-9847-8 (vol. 6)   1-4144-9847-0 (vol. 6)

This title is also available as an e-book.
ISBN-13: 978-1-4144-9848-5   ISBN-10: 1-4144-9848-9
Contact your Gale, a part of Cengage Learning sales representative for ordering
information.

Printed in China
1 2 3 4 5 6 7 17 16 15 14 13

Contents

VOLUME 1: THE ANCIENT WORLD

Prehistory

Ancient Egypt

India

Ancient Greece

VOLUME 2: EARLY CULTURES ACROSS THE GLOBE

Early Asian Cultures

Oceania

Native American Cultures

Mayans, Aztecs, and Incas

African Cultures

VOLUME 3: EUROPEAN CULTURE FROM THE RENAISSANCE TO THE MODERN ERA

The Fifteenth Century

The Sixteenth Century

The Seventeenth Century

Fashion, Costume and Culture, 2nd edition

The Nineteenth Century

VOLUME 4: MODERN WORLD PART I: 1900 TO 1945

1900–18

VOLUME 5: MODERN WORLD PART II: 1946 TO 1999

1946–60

Post–World War II: 1946–60 .... **829**

VOLUME 6: MODERN WORLD PART III: 2000 TO 2012 AND RELIGIOUS VESTMENTS

Fashion, Costume and Culture, 2nd edition

Fashion, Costume and Culture, 2nd edition

Entries by Alphabetical Order

Q

R

S

Entries by Topic Category

Reader's Guide

Fashion, Costume, and Culture: Clothing, Headwear, Body Decorations, and Footwear through the Ages, Second Edition provides a broad overview of costume traditions of diverse cultures from prehistoric times to the present day. The six-volume set explores various items of human decoration and adornment, ranging from togas to turbans, necklaces to tennis shoes, and discusses why and how they were created, the people who made them, and their uses. More than just a description of what people wore and why, this set also describes how clothing, headwear, body decorations, and footwear reflect different cultural, religious, and societal beliefs.

Volume 1 covers the ancient world, including prehistoric man and the ancient cultures of Egypt, Mesopotamia, India, Greece, and Rome. Key issues covered in this volume include the early use of animal skins as garments, the introduction of fabric as the primary human body covering, and the development of distinct cultural traditions for draped and fitted garments.

Volume 2 looks at the transition from the ancient world to the Middle Ages, focusing on the Asian cultures of China and Japan, the Byzantine Empire, the nomadic and barbarian cultures of early Europe, and Europe in the formative Middle Ages. This volume also highlights several of the ancient cultures of North America, South and Central America, and Africa that were encountered by Europeans during the Age of Exploration that began in the fifteenth century.

Volumes 3 through 5 offer chronological coverage of the development of costume and fashion in the West. Volume 3 features the costume traditions of the developing European nation-states in the fifteenth through the nineteenth centuries, and looks at the importance of the royal courts in introducing clothing styles and the shift from home-based garmentmaking to shop-based and then factory-based industry.

Volumes 4 and 5 cover Western history in the twentieth century. These volumes trace the rise of the fashion designer as the primary creator of new clothing styles, chart the impact of technology on costume traditions, and present the innovations made possible by the introduction of new synthetic, or man-made, materials. Perhaps most importantly, Volumes 4 and 5 discuss what is sometimes referred to as the democratization of fashion. At beginning of the century, high quality, stylish clothes were designed by and made available to a privileged elite; by the middle to end of the century, well-made clothes were widely available in the West, and new styles came from creative and usually youth-oriented cultural groups as often as they did from designers.

Volume 6 contains two distinct sections. The first part of the book continues the chronology of style and culture by discussing twenty-first century fashion. Overarching themes include the progressive use of technology, a heightened awareness of environmentally-conscious issues, and a rise in the culture of celebrity. The second part of volume 6 covers the clothing and accessories associated with the major religions of the world. The symbolism of certain garments is explained, and the way in which specific objects and vestments define and shape each particular belief system is also covered.

Organization

Fashion, Costume, and Culture, Second Edition is organized into twenty-seven chapters, focusing on specific cultural traditions or on a specific chronological period in history. Each of these chapters share the following components:

- A chapter introduction, which discusses the general historical framework for the chapter and highlights the major social and economic factors that relate to the development of costume traditions.
- Four sections that cover Clothing, Headwear, Body Decorations, and Footwear. Each of these sections opens with an overview that discusses general trends within the broader category, and nearly every section contains one or more essays on specific garments or trends that were important during the period.

Each chapter introduction and individual essay in *Fashion, Costume, and Culture,* Second Edition includes a For More Information section listing sources—books, articles, and Web sites—containing additional information on fashion and the people and events it addresses. Some essays also contain *See also* references that direct the reader to other essays within the set that can offer more information on this or related items.

Bringing the text to life are more than 390 color or black-and-white photos and maps, while numerous sidebar boxes offer additional insight into the people, places, and happenings that influenced fashion throughout the years. Other features include tables of contents listing the contents of all six volumes, listing the entries by alphabetical order, and listing entries by category. Rounding out the set are a timeline of important events in fashion history, a words to know section defining terms used throughout the set, a bibliography of general fashion sources, including notable Web sites, and a comprehensive subject index, which provides easy access to the subjects discussed throughout *Fashion, Costume, and Culture,* Second Edition.

Acknowledgements

Many thanks to the following advisors who provided valuable comments and suggestions for the first edition of *Fashion, Costume, and Culture* (their professional affiliation at the time of the publication of the first edition is noted): Ginny Chaussee, Retired Media Specialist, Mountain Pointe High School, Phoenix, Arizona; Carol Keeler, Media Specialist, Detroit Country Day Upper School, Beverly Hills, Michigan; Nina Levine, Library Media Specialist, Blue Mountain Middle School, Cortlandt Manor, New York; and Bonnie Raasch, Media Specialist, C. B. Vernon Middle School, Marion, Iowa.

We also owe a great deal to the writers of the first edition who have helped us create the hundreds of essays in this book (the contributors page reprints their background at the time of the first edition): Sara Pendergast, Tom Pendergast, Tina Gianoulis, Rob Edelman, Bob Schnakenberg, Audrey Kupferberg, and Carol Brennan. The editors of the first edition would also like to thank the staffs of two libraries, at the University of Washington and the Sno-Isle Regional Library, for allowing us to ransack and hold hostage their costume collections for months at a time.

We cannot help but mention the great debt we owe to the costume historians whose works we have consulted, and whose names appear again and again in the bibliographies of the essays. We sincerely hope that this collection pays tribute to and furthers their collective production of knowledge.

Comments and Suggestions

We welcome your comments on *Fashion, Costume, and Culture,* Second Edition as well as your suggestions for topics to be featured in the future editions. Please write to: Editor, *Fashion, Costume, and Culture,* U•X•L, 27500 Drake Rd., Farmington Hills, MI 48331-3535; call toll-free: 800-877-4253; fax to 248-414-5043; or send e-mail via www.gale.com.

Contributors

Carol Brennan. Freelance writer, Grosse Pointe, MI.

Rob Edelman. Instructor, State University of New York at Albany. Author, *Baseball on the Web* (1997) and *The Great Baseball Films* (1994). Co-author, *Mertzes* (1999); and *Angela Lansbury: A Life on Stage and Screen* (1996). Contributing editor, *Leonard Maltin's Move & Video Guide, Leonard Maltin's Movie Encyclopedia,* and *Leonard Maltin's Family Viewing Guide.* Contributing writer, *International Dictionary of Films and Filmmakers* (2000); *St. James Encyclopedia of Popular Culture* (2000); *Women Filmmakers & Their Films* (1998); *The Political Companion to American Film* (1994); and *Total Baseball* (1989). Film commentator, WAMC (Northeast) Public Radio.

Alicia Baker Elley. Freelance writer/editor. Contributing writer/editor, *American Eras: Primary Sources* (2012); *International Director of Company Histories* (2010–12); *African American Eras* (2009); and *Dictionary of Literary Biography* (2008).

Tina Gianoulis. Freelance writer. Contributing writer, *World War I Reference Library* (2002); *Constitutional Amendments: From Freedom of Speech to Flag Burning* (2001); *International Dictionary of Films and Filmmakers* (2000); *St. James Encyclopedia of Popular Culture* (2000); and mystories.com, a daytime drama Web site (1997–98).

Hilary Hylton. Freelance writer and author based in Austin, Texas. *TIME*; *Insiders' Guide to Austin* (2011); *Corporate Disasters: What Went Wrong and Why; Business Insights: Global; Gale Encyclopedia of Electronic Commerce; Gale International Directory of Company Histories, Vol. 140; Mexico: A Texas Monthly Guidebook* (1991).

Drew D. Johnson. Writer and editor living in Austin, Texas. Cofounder of Anaxos, Inc. Publications include: *Encyclopedia of Management; Kidding Around Austin; McGraw-Hill LSAT 2013; Spanish/English Terms for Nurses; Homework Heroes.*

Atley Jonas. Canadian business writer and editor based in Japan; MBA specialized in global management and communications. Contributing writer and editor for works including: *Gale E-Commerce Sourcebook,* (2011); *Corporate Disasters: What Went Wrong and Why* (2012); and *International Directory of Company Histories* (2012).

Audrey Kupferberg. Film consultant and archivist. Instructor, State University of New York at Albany. Co-author, *Matthau: A Life* (2002); *Meet the Mertzes* (1999); and *Angela Lansbury: A Life on Stage and Screen* (1996). Contributing editor, *Leonard Maltin's Family Viewing Guide.* Contributing writer, *St. James Encyclopedia of Popular Culture* (2000). Editor, *Rhythm* (2001), a magazine of world music and global culture.

Sara Pendergast. President, Full Circle Editorial. Vice president, Group 3 Editorial. Co-editor, *St. James Encyclopedia of Popular Culture* (2000). Co-author, *World War I Reference Library* (2002), among other publications.

Tom Pendergast. Editorial director, Full Circle Editorial. Ph.D., American studies, Purdue University. Author, *Creating the Modern Man: American Magazines and Consumer Culture* (2000). Co-editor, *St. James Encyclopedia of Popular Culture* (2000).

Christine Purfield. Freelance writer. Contributing writer, *International Directory of Company Histories* (2012); *Fashion, Costume, and Culture,* Second Edition (2012);

Robert E. Schnakenberg. Senior writer, History Book Club. Author, *The Encyclopedia Shatnerica* (1998).

Greg Wilson. Freelance literature and popular culture writer. Contributing writer, *Literary Newsmakers for Students* (2006), *UXL Encyclopedia of World Mythology* (2009), *Top Stories 2010: Behind the Headlines* (2011), *Bowling, Beatniks, and Bell-Bottoms: Pop Culture of 20th and 21st Century America* (2012).

Timeline

The beginning of human life Early humans wrap themselves in animal hides for warmth.

c. 10,000 B.C.E. Tattooing is practiced on the Japanese islands, in the Jomon period (c. 10,000–300 B.C.E.). Similarly scarification has been practiced since ancient times in Oceania and Africa to make a person's body more beautiful or signify a person's rank in society.

c. 3100 B.C.E. Egyptians weave a plant called flax into a light cloth called linen and made dresses and loincloths from it.

c. 3000 B.C.E. Men and women in the Middle East, Africa, and the Far East have wrapped turbans on their heads since ancient times, and the turban continues to be popular with both men and women in many modern cultures.

c. 2600 B.C.E. to 900 C.E. Ancient Mayans, whose civilization flourishes in Belize and on the Yucatan Peninsula in Mexico, flatten the heads of the children of wealthy and powerful members of society. The children's heads are squeezed between two boards to elongate their skulls into a shape that looks very similar to an ear of corn.

c. 2500 B.C.E. Indians wear a wrapped style of trousers called a dhoti and a skirt-like lower body covering called a lungi. At the same time Indian women begin to adorn themselves in the wrapped dress style called a sari.

liii

c. 1500 B.C.E. Egyptian men adopt the tunic as an upper body covering when Egypt conquers Syria.

c. 27 B.C.E.–476 C.E. Roman soldiers, especially horsemen, adopt the trousers, or feminalia, of the nomadic tribes they encounter on the outskirts of the Roman Empire.

Sixth and fifth centuries B.C.E. The doric chiton becomes one of the most popular garments for both men and women in ancient Greece.

Fifth century B.C.E. The toga, a wrapped garment, is favored by Romans.

c. 476 Upper-class men, and sometimes women, in the Byzantine Empire (476–1453 C.E.) wear a long, flowing robe-like overgarment called a dalmatica developed from the tunic.

c. 900 Young Chinese girls tightly bind their feet to keep them small, a sign of beauty for a time in Chinese culture. The practice was outlawed in 1911.

c. 1100–1500 The cote, a long robe worn by both men and women, and its descendant, the cotehardie, are among the most common garments of the late Middle Ages.

1392 Kimonos are first worn in China as an undergarment. The word "kimono" later came to be used to describe the native dress of Japan in the nineteenth century.

1470 The first farthingales, or hoops worn under a skirt to hold it out away from the body, are worn in Spain and are called vertugados. These farthingales become popular in France and England and are later known as the Spanish farthingale.

Fifteenth century and sixteenth century The doublet—a slightly padded short overshirt, usually buttoned down the front, with or without sleeves—becomes an essential men's garment.

Late fifteenth through the sixteenth century The ruff, a wide pleated collar, often stiffened with starch or wire, is worn by wealthy men and women of the time.

Sixteenth century Worn underneath clothing, corsets squeeze and mold women's bodies into the correct shape to fit changing fashions of dress.

Seventeenth century The Kuba people, living in the present-day nation of the Democratic Republic of the Congo, weave a decorative cloth called Kuba cloth. An entire social group of men and women is involved in the production of the cloth, from gathering the fibers, weaving the cloth, and dyeing the decorative strands, to applying the embroidery, appliqué, or patchwork.

1643 French courtiers begin wearing wigs to copy the long curly hair of the sixteen-year-old king, Louis XIV. The fashion for long wigs continues later when, at the age of thirty-five, Louis begins to cover his thinning hair with wigs to maintain his beloved style.

Eighteenth century The French Revolution (1789–99) destroys the French monarchy and makes ankle-length trousers fashionable attire for all men. Trousers come to symbolize the ideas of the Revolution, an effort to make French people more equal, and soon men of all classes are wearing long trousers.

1778 À la Belle Poule, a huge hairstyle commemorating the victory of a French ship over an English ship in 1778, features an enormous pile of curled and powdered hair stretched over a frame affixed to the top of a woman's head. The hair is decorated with a model of the ship in full sail.

1849 Dark blue, heavy-duty cotton pants—known as blue jeans—are created as work pants for the gold miners of the 1849 California gold rush.

1868 A sturdy canvas and rubber shoe called a croquet sandal is introduced and sells for six dollars a pair, making it too expensive for all but the very wealthy. The shoe later became known as the tennis shoe.

1870 A French hairstylist named Marcel Grateau invents the first long-lasting hair waving technique using a heated iron to give hair curls that lasts for days.

Late 1800s to early 1900s The feathered war bonnet, traditional to only a small number of Native American tribes, becomes known as a typical Native American headdress with the help of Buffalo

Bill Cody's Wild West Show, which features theatrical representations of the Indians and cowboys of the American West and travels throughout America and parts of Europe.

1900s Loose, floppy, two-legged undergarments for women, bloomers start a trend toward less restrictive clothing for women, including clothing that allows them to ride bicycles, play tennis, and to take part in other sport activities.

1915 American inventor T.L. Williams develops a cake of mascara and a brush to darken the lashes and sells them through the mail under the name Maybelline.

1920s Advances in paint technology allow the creation of a hard durable paint and fuel an increase in the popularity of colored polish for fingernails and toenails. During this same period women begin wearing short, bobbed hairstyles.

1930s Popular as a shirt for tennis, golf, and other sport activities for decades, the polo shirt becomes the most popular leisure shirt for men.

1939 For the first time, *Vogue,* the respected fashion magazine, pictures women in trousers.

1945 Servicemen returning home from World War II (1939–45) continue to wear the T-shirts they had been issued as undershirts during the war and soon the T-shirt becomes an acceptable casual outershirt.

1946 The bikini, a two-piece bathing suit, is developed and named after a group of coral islands in the Pacific Ocean.

1950s The gray flannel suit becomes the most common outfit worn by men working at desk jobs in office buildings.

1957 Liquid mascara is sold at retail stores in tubes with a brush inside.

1960s and 1970s The afro, featuring a person's naturally curly hair trimmed in a full, evenly round shape around the head, is the most popular hairstyle among African Americans.

c. 1965 Women begin wearing miniskirts with hemlines hitting at mid-thigh or above.

1980s Power dressing becomes a trend toward wearing expensive, designer clothing for work.

1990s Casual Fridays becomes the name given to the practice of allowing employees to dress informally on the last day of the work week.

1990s Grunge, a trend for wearing old, sometimes stained or ripped clothing, becomes a fashion sensation and prompts designers to sell simple flannel shirts for prices in excess of one thousand dollars.

2000s Versions of clothing available during the 1960s and 1970s, such as bell-bottom jeans and the peasant look, return to fashion as "retro fashions."

2010s The availability of the Internet influences style, allowing people to see celebrities they admire online (via computer or smartphone) and then purchase similar clothing moments later.

Words to Know

Appliqué: An ornament sewn, embroidered, or glued onto a garment.

Bias cut: A fabric cut diagonally across the weave to create a softly draped garment.

Bodice: The part of a woman's garment that covers her torso from neck to waist.

Bombast: Padding used to increase the width or add bulk to the general silhouette of a garment.

Brim: The edge of a hat that projects outward away from the head.

Brocade: A fabric woven with a raised pattern over the entire surface.

Collar: The part of a shirt that surrounds the neck.

Crown: The portion of a hat that covers the top of the head; may also refer to the top part of the head.

Cuff: A piece of fabric sewn at the bottom of a sleeve.

Double-breasted: A style of jacket in which one side (usually the left) overlaps in the front of the other side, fastens at the waist with a vertical row of buttons, and has another row of buttons on the opposite side that is purely decorative.

Embroidery: Needlework designs on the surface of a fabric, added for decoration.

Garment: Any article of clothing.

Hemline: The bottom edge of a skirt, jacket, dress, or other garment.
Hide: The pelt of an animal with the fur intact.

Instep: The upper surface of the arched middle portion of the human foot in front of the ankle joint.

Jersey: A knitted fabric usually made of wool or cotton.

Lapel: One of the two flaps that extend down from the collar of a coat or jacket and fold back against the chest.

Lasts: The foot-shaped forms or molds that are used to give shape to shoes in the process of shoemaking.

Leather: The skin or hide of an animal cleaned and treated to soften it and preserve it from decay.

Linen: A fabric woven from the fibers of the flax plant. Linen was one of the first woven fabrics.

Mule: A shoe without a covering or strap around the heel of the foot.

Muslin: A thin cotton fabric.

Patent Leather: Leather varnished and buffed to a high shine.

Placket: A slit in a dress, blouse, or skirt.

Pleat: A decorative feature on a garment in which fabric has been doubled over, pressed, and stitched in place.

Queue: A ponytail of hair gathered at the back of a wig with a band.

Ready-to-wear: Clothing manufactured in standard sizes and sold to customers without custom alterations.

Silhouette: The general shape or outline of the human body.

Single-breasted: A jacket fastened down the front with a single row of buttons.

Sole: The bottom of a shoe, covering the bottom of the foot.

Straights: The forms, or lasts, used to make the soles of shoes without differentiating between the left and right feet.

Suede: Skin from a young goat, called kidskin or calfskin, buffed to a velvet-like finish.

Synthetic: A term used to describe chemically made fabrics, such as nylon, acrylic, polyester, and vinyl.

Taffeta: A shiny, smooth fabric woven of silk or other materials.

Textile: A cloth or fabric, especially when woven or knitted.

Throat: The opening of a shoe at the instep.

Twill: A fabric with a diagonal line pattern woven onto the surface.

Upper: The parts of a shoe above the sole.

Velvet: A fabric with a short, plush pile of silk, cotton, or other material.

Wig: A head covering worn to conceal the hair or to cover a bald head.

From Riches to Ruin: 1900–18

The first two decades of the twentieth century saw dramatic changes in the political, social, and economic life in the West. The prosperity that characterized life at the turn of the twentieth century was largely the result of industrialization, a long historic process that had introduced factory production to many major industries, including mining, manufacturing, and the production of clothing. Industrialization had brought great wealth to the major powers of the world, making Great Britain, Germany, France, and the United States the most prosperous countries on earth. Yet it also allowed these countries to create powerful armies. When these armies clashed in World War I (1914–18), they participated in one of the bloodiest wars in history.

Industrialization, prosperity, and social change

People living in the major Western countries at the turn of the twentieth century were more prosperous than at any time in history. The rise of factory production had stimulated the economies of the West, creating giant corporations headed by extremely wealthy businessmen. The wealth created by modern economies went primarily to rich factory owners and bankers, but it also raised the living standards of people throughout the West. The middle classes grew larger in the 1900s and became an increasingly important political class. They exerted a great influence on politics, especially in the United States. Industrialization also made the lives of the working classes less desperate, if still difficult. Workers in large cities organized themselves into labor unions, groups of people who used their numbers to gain influence in the economy and in politics. No longer did the wealthy few control politics in the West; in the twentieth century all classes had some influence.

The increasing influence of the middle and working classes led to major social changes at the beginning of the new century. First, middle-class

Civilian Dress in Wartime

World War I (1914–18) brought many changes to the countries involved. Whether the war was fought on their soil or their troops were sent abroad to fight, people in Germany, Austria, France, Great Britain, Russia, the United States, Canada, and other countries saw many changes in their daily lives, including the way they dressed. Jobs and leisure time became filled with war-related activities, and different clothing was needed for those activities. Politics inspired citizens to wear certain items of clothing to show agreement or disagreement with their government, while hardship dictated that certain materials were unavailable to make clothes. The clothing of civilians, or nonsoldiers, during World War I reflected not only the effects of the war itself, but also the influence of an era of great social change.

Dressing for War

As the warring countries prepared to battle, large numbers of men joined the military, and women all over Europe and the United States began to work in public jobs, such as streetcar drivers and conductors, postal workers, secretaries, lamplighters, and chimney sweeps. In Britain, "land girls" worked on farms, and more than 700,000 women worked in military equipment factories. Even upper-class women who did not need paying jobs often did war-related volunteer work. These workers complained that the heavy, bulky skirts and underclothes that they wore were too cumbersome for their physically active jobs. They soon wore loose blouses over trousers or overalls, which were often the most practical working clothes.

Another factor that changed the way people dressed was the need to restrict certain materials for military use. Long, flowing skirts used too much fabric and corsets used steel, so these garments quickly went out of fashion. Women wore the new style of soft elastic corsets, called

women led successful campaigns for increased rights, including suffrage (the right to vote) and the right to work. Though women were not yet viewed as social equals to men, they were on their way. Secondly, the increase in literate people, or people able to read, with excess income that they were looking to spend allowed for the creation of popular culture, including magazines, movies, and later radio and even television. These new forms of entertainment spread information very quickly, including information about politics and fashion. These forms of entertainment brought people closer, since people in different states and even different countries could read the same magazines, watch the same movies, and wear the same clothes. Another factor bringing people closer together was the automobile, which grew from a novelty to a necessity in the first twenty years of the century.

girdles, and skirts hemmed to mid-calf to show support for the war effort. These clothes were also much easier to move around in.

National Standard Dress

In 1918 the British government introduced a new garment called a "National Standard Dress," a simple loose, mid-calf dress made with no hooks and eyes. Because cotton and wool were needed for the war effort, the National Standard Dress was made from silk and was intended to be an all-purpose dress that could be worn for any occasion, any time of day or evening. Though the National Standard Dress was never universally popular, it did point out a general trend toward less formal styles. During the war both men and women began to dress less formally than before and to wear the same clothes for different purposes. Men, for example, first began wearing a simply designed suit for many occasions, rather than

different kinds of suits for morning, dinner, and evening.

Because of the patriotic atmosphere encouraged by the war, it became fashionable to wear clothes that looked military. Both women and men wore bits of military trim, such as braid and belts with buckles. Other items were adapted from military wear, such as trench coats, which were designed with many similarities to uniforms, such as epaulets, straps on the shoulders, and metal rings for attaching weapons. German air force pilots started a fashion by cutting off the tails of their long leather coats so they would fit more easily into an airplane cockpit, and thousands began copying the new "bomber jackets."

Once the war ended in 1918 a wider variety of fashions became available again. However, the more practical clothing worn by women during the war and the dashing style adopted by many men carried over into the next decade.

World War I

Despite rising prosperity, social liberation, and the growth of popular culture, the differing political goals of the European powers soon led to a disastrous war. World War I pitted Germany, Austria, and their allies against France, Great Britain, Russia, the United States, Canada, and their allies. The great capability of modern industry was turned toward war, and factories produced the machine guns, tanks, and airplanes that made killing more efficient than ever before. Millions died in the war, and the economies of the European powers were severely damaged, leaving the United States as the most powerful country in the world. The war also brought great social change, for it brought many women into the workplace to replace the male workers who went overseas to fight.

Industrialization, the women's movement, the rise of popular culture, and the war each had an impact on the world of fashion. While the clothing customs of the first years of the century were dominated by the interests of Europe's wealthiest people, clothing soon changed to reflect the diverse tastes of consumers from all social classes. By the end of World War I clothing customs in the West had entered the modern era.

For More Information

Blanke, David. *The 1910s*. Westport, CT: Greenwood Press, 2002.

Feinstein, Stephen. *The 1900s, from Teddy Roosevelt to Flying Machines*. Berkeley Heights, NJ: Enslow, 2001.

Immell, Myra H., ed. *The 1900s*. San Diego, CA: Greenhaven Press, 2000.

Kennedy, David M. *Over Here: The First World War and American Society*. New York: Oxford University Press, 1980.

Peacock, John. *Fashion since 1900: the complete sourcebook*. London, England: Thames and Hudson, 2007.

Uschan, Michael V. *The 1910s*. San Diego, CA: Lucent Books, 1999.

Woog, Adam. *The 1900s*. San Diego, CA: Lucent Books, 1999.

Wukovits, John F. *The 1910s*. San Diego, CA: Greenhaven Press, 2000.

Clothing, 1900–18

The period from the turn of the twentieth century to the end of World War I (1914–18) was one of great transition in the world of fashion. Not only did styles for women undergo a dramatic shift in their basic silhouette, or shape, but the very system through which new styles were introduced and popularized also changed. Paris, France, was the center of the world of fashion, but more and more people got their fashion ideas from magazines and their fashionable clothes, ready-to-wear, from department stores close to home. Social changes, especially the increasing liberation of women and the coming of war, also had a dramatic impact on fashion. These and other changes made this the period in which the fashion system, or the way that new styles were created and adopted by people, truly began to resemble what we know today.

The changing fashion system

Ever since the end of the Middle Ages (c. 500–c. 1500), when rich kings and queens secured power and were surrounded by wealthy nobles, European clothing traditions had been sharply split between the wealthy and the poor and middle classes. The wealthy were concerned with fashion, following the latest clothing styles, usually those set by royalty, and wearing the richest and most luxurious garments available. Everyone else wore simple, everyday apparel that was chosen for its durability and its utility. Over time, as incomes increased, more and more people became concerned with fashion, but true fashion, with frequent changes and expensive and luxurious fabrics, remained only for the very wealthy. In the first years of the twentieth century, however, the system began to change.

1912   Costumes Parisiens   32

*Robe de Soie de Chine bordée de Chinchilla. Manteau de velours
Citron vert à grand Col et parements de Chinchilla, gland d'argent.*

*A coat and dress ensemble
popular in Western countries
during the first decades
of the twentieth century.*
© VICTORIA & ALBERT MUSEUM,
LONDON UK/THE BRIDGEMAN
ART LIBRARY.

At the dawn of the twentieth century, Paris was the center of the fashion world. Clothing designers from Paris introduced clothing at seasonal shows and sold clothes to the wealthiest people in Europe and the United States. Increasingly, however, these fashions began to reach more and more people. Dressmakers outside of Paris might buy an expensive gown, take it apart, and make a pattern, or design to make a dress, which they sold, allowing the dress to be reproduced. Publishers began to sell pattern books of fashionable clothes that allowed people to make the clothes at home if they were good sewers. Soon, department stores, which were becoming popular throughout the West, also began to sew and sell dresses modeled on the latest Paris fashions.

Ready-to-wear

These changes were small compared to the introduction of ready-to-wear clothing. In the past all clothing had been made by hand in the home, or by tailors for the upper classes. But the introduction of the sewing machine combined with the factory system allowed for the mass production of clothing in the nineteenth century. Men's clothing was the first to be mass-produced in a variety of different sizes. This form of clothing was called ready-to-wear. By the end of the nineteenth century men could go into a store and buy ready-to-wear trousers, shirts, or jackets, but women still had to buy cloth and sew the clothes themselves. By the first years of the twentieth century, ready-to-wear clothing was available to women, too.

The first widely available ready-to-wear garment for women was the shirtwaist, a blouse that was worn with a long, flowing skirt. Designers in Paris might offer a beautiful shirtwaist, and before too long a factory in Massachusetts would be making a close copy that could be purchased at the local department store for a much lower price. Though most clothing, and certainly the more luxurious gowns of the day, was still made at home or by a skilled tailor, ready-to-wear clothing became an important industry in the 1900s and 1910s.

Social change and fashion

The clothing styles that dominated the first years of the twentieth century were carried over from the late nineteenth century. Long flowing dresses with highly decorated sleeves were common for women and were worn with elaborate hats. While the details of these dresses changed from season to season, the essential outline of the woman's figure, or her silhouette, remained in the S-shape that was so fashionable at the turn of the century. Rigid corsets, or stiffened undergarments, gave the woman a prominent chest, a very narrow waist, and extended buttocks, bolstered with padding. This silhouette was uncomfortable and made movement difficult.

This restrictive women's clothing was increasingly at odds with the way women viewed their lives. Across Europe and in the United States, women began to resist the confining social systems that gave men more power and kept women in the home. They began to push for more rights, such as the right to vote and the right to work outside the home. Restrictive, uncomfortable clothes were soon identified with restrictive social systems, and they too were rejected. After about 1908 women quit wearing confining corsets and impractical long gowns. They sought out garments that had a more natural shape, such as a tube-shaped dress or a simple skirt and shirtwaist combination. Clothing designers followed suit and soon began to produce a range of clothing that was more natural and comfortable.

The feeling of liberation that came to women's clothing, especially in the 1910s, came from other directions as well. The widespread popularity of motoring, or riding in automobiles, created a need for practical clothing that wouldn't get ruined by dust and wind. Also, as sports such as tennis and golf opened up to women, clothes changed to allow women to move more freely. The rising length of women's skirts was a big sign that women's clothes were becoming more practical.

World War I

One of the biggest social factors that influenced fashion was World War I. World War I drained the resources of every country involved, including the major European powers and the United States and Canada.

Paul Poiret

During the years before World War I (1914–18), Paul Poiret (1879–1944) earned acclaim for designing flamboyant, brightly colored women's clothing. He was inspired by a range of preexisting styles, from Oriental and Greco-Roman designs to Russian peasant costumes, as well as by the fine and decorative arts.

Poiret was born in Paris, France, and his family operated a cloth business. As a child he was fascinated by the theater and the fine arts. In 1896 he was hired by fashion designer Jacques Doucet (1853–1929), proprietor of one of the era's top Paris fashion houses. While working for Doucet, he earned acclaim by designing stage costumes for some of the period's most illustrious French actresses, including Sarah Bernhardt (1844–1923) and Réjane (1857–1920). He also worked at Maison Worth, another celebrated Paris-based design house. In 1904 Poiret opened his own design firm, which he named La Maison Poiret, or the House of Poiret.

At the time women regularly wore corsets, stiff, tight-fitting undergarments. Poiret freed women from their corsets and dressed them in a variety of clothing: tubular, sheath-like dresses; elegant, highly ornamental kimonos, loose-fitting, wide-sleeved robes; long tunic dresses; harem pants (women's pants featuring full legs that come together at the ankle); and hobble skirts (long skirts that come in tight at the ankles). In place of corsets Poiret endorsed the wearing of brassieres as women's underwear.

To Poiret color and ornament were just as important as the cut of a garment. He worked with various Paris-based painters and illustrators to create stylish, brightly colored fashion illustrations and textile print designs. Poiret befriended many artists, and preferred modern French painting at a time when it had not yet won acceptance. He collected the work of those who would become the era's leading artists, among them Pablo Picasso (1881–1973), Henri Matisse (1869–1954), and Francis Picabia (1879–1953).

In 1908 Poiret began printing the designs he commissioned in limited-edition catalogs, which he sent to his customers. The manner in which these catalogs were laid out influenced the evolution of the fashion magazine. In 1911 Poiret marketed one of the first designer perfumes, which he named Rosine. Under the Rosine name he also sold lotions and other cosmetic products. Then in 1912 he opened Atelier Martine, where he sold the fabrics and wallpaper created by his students at Paris's École Martine, a school of decorative arts.

During the 1920s fashion styles became less ornate and a new generation of designers came into favor. Poiret did not adapt his work to the changing tastes, and his business no longer flourished. Rosine did not survive the Great Depression, and by the time Poiret died in 1944 he had lost his money, had long been in ill health, and was practically forgotten. If Poiret were alive today, however, he might be happy to know that his brand was revived in 1991 by Marie Hélène Rogeon, whose great-grandfather worked with Poiret. The modern perfumes by Rosine are new creations though, and not revivals of the original formulations by Poiret. Rosine still does make lotions, creams, and perfumed candles.

Fabrics and materials used for clothing were rationed, and clothing became simpler and less ornamented as a result. Perhaps the biggest impact was on women's dresses, which were made with far less material than ever before. The slim profile demanded by the war became the dominant fashion of the 1920s. The war also brought more women into the workplace than ever before, and women wore new clothing, including the once-forbidden trousers, in the workplace that they later adopted for regular use.

Men's clothing

Men's clothing in general changed much less frequently and less dramatically than women's clothing. Standard wear for men in nonmanual work was the sack suit, or three-piece suit, usually worn with a shirt with a detachable collar, while working-class men generally wore trousers and a button-down shirt. These outfits didn't change on a seasonal basis like women's, though men's suits did see a slimming in profile that came in about 1908, around the same time as changes in the women's silhouette. Men took advantage of the greater availability of ready-to-wear clothing, especially the newer, less restrictive forms of underwear that replaced the union suit, an undergarment that was shirt and drawers in one. They also enjoyed the looser, more casual clothes created for use while playing sports or motoring. While Paris was the center of women's fashion, London, England, was the center for men.

The years from 1900 to 1918 were filled with many more important influences on clothing customs, including the growing popularity of fashion magazines, the importance of advertising in shaping people's ideas about clothing, the rise in the status of the fashion designer as a trendsetter, and the influence of trends in art and dance.

For More Information

Ewing, Elizabeth. *History of Twentieth Century Fashion*. Revised by Alice Mackrell. Lanham, MD: Barnes and Noble Books, 1992.

Laver, James. *Costume and Fashion: A Concise History*. 4th ed. London, England: Thames and Hudson, 2002.

"Les Parfums de Rosine Perfumes and Colognes." *Fragrantica*. http://www.fragrantica.com/designers/Les-Parfums-de-Rosine.html (accessed on September 2, 2012).

Payne, Blanche, Geitel Winakor, and Jane Farrell-Beck. *The History of Costume*. 2nd ed. New York: HarperCollins, 1992.

Bloomers

Bloomers were baggy underpants for women, usually made of cotton, which gathered at the waist and below at the knees. Because they were worn under long, slightly loose A-line skirts and dresses, the leggings also could hang on the legs in an ungathered fashion, falling halfway between the knees and the ankles. They were worn by women during the early decades of the twentieth century but went out of style when skirt lengths became shorter at the end of the 1910s.

The first attributable instance of bloomers being worn publicly was by early women's rights activist Elizabeth Smith Miller. On a trip to Europe, she saw "Turkish pantaloons" being worn, and thought that she would introduce the concept to her cousin and women's rights advocate, Elizabeth Cady Stanton. Stanton, who was friends with still another activist, Amelia Jenks Bloomer (1818–1894), introduced the garment to her. The term bloomer bears Bloomer's name because she popularized the garment by wearing it herself, and also used her position as editor of *Lily* magazine to promote it. Bloomer wanted women to wear clothing that promoted freedom of movement, so she appeared in public in the knee-length, loose-fitting pants. During her lifetime, most people made fun of Bloomer's progressive fashion statement. When bloomers were introduced to mainstream women as a form of comfortable undergarment in the late 1800s, the reception at first was controversial. Many men and women viewed the underwear as unnatural to a woman's form, as it had separate leg coverings. These critics preferred that women wear only layers of petticoats around their bodies.

Eventually Stanton abandoned wearing the style herself, due to intense pressure and public scrutiny. In her diary she wrote, "People would stare, many make rude remarks, boys follow in crowds, with jeers and laughter, so that gentlemen in attendance would feel it their duty to show fight, unless they had sufficient self-control to show the even tenor of their way…" Amelia Bloomer remained steadfast, however, and continued wearing the controversial garment.

Eventually, women were attracted to the comfort and warmth of bloomers. As women became more active in sports, and as they ventured from the home into the workforce, they also were drawn to the practicality of bloomers. As skirts became less full and flowed more in tune with the natural shape of a woman, items such as bloomers served as modest undergarments that moved along with the curves of the lower body.

Women were drawn to the practicality of bloomers as they became more active in sports. © HAGLEY MUSEUM & LIBRARY, WILMINGTON, DELAWARE, USA/THE BRIDGEMAN ART LIBRARY

By the early 1900s bloomers had become common undergarments for women,

At this time bloomers also were worn as outer garments by outgoing, sporting women. They were mass manufactured in durable heavy cotton for schoolgirls to wear while playing sports in school gymnasiums. Outerwear bloomers particularly were scoffed at when worn by women who were enjoying the controversial new sport of bicycling. At that time the idea of a woman wearing a split-legged pants-type garment in public was considered by many to be indecent.

Bloomers were made of various fabrics. Working women and schoolgirls wore lightweight cotton bloomers in warm weather and heavier flannel bloomers in the cold. Bloomers for the wealthier classes were made of white or pastel silk; some were hand-laced or embroidered. In the days before rubberized fabrics such as elastic, the gatherings at the waist and knees were accomplished by tying ribbons or fastening buttons to the garment. The knee borders of bloomers were often given decorative trim such as lace or crocheted fabric through which colorful ribbons ran. To make using the bathroom easier some styles of bloomers were split at the crotch, while others had back seat flaps that were fastened to the main garment with buttons.

Along with bloomers, women wore several other undergarments during this period. On their upper bodies they wore chemises, loose-fitting undershirts of soft cotton or silk. Atop the bloomers and chemise came the corset, which covered the breasts and extended down to the hips. By 1908 cumbersome corsets were being replaced by less restrictive brassieres that supported only the breasts.

SEE ALSO *Volume 3, Seventeenth Century: Petticoats; Volume 3, Eighteenth Century: Corsets; Volume 3, Nineteenth Century: Bloomers Volume 4, 1900–18: Brassiere*

For More Information

Cunnington, C. Willett, and Phyllis Cunnington. *The History of Underclothes.* New York: Gordon Press, 1979.

"Elizabeth Smith Miller." *New York History Net.* http://www.nyhistory.com/gerritsmith/esm.htm (accessed on September 3, 2002).

"The First of the Flappers." *Literary Digest,* May 13, 1922. http://www.oldmagazinearticles.com/Elizabeth_Cady_Stanton_and_Amelia_Bloomer_article (accessed on September 3, 2002).

Robbins, Sarah. "Rebel without a Skirt—Cultural Context." *Women's Work in the Long 19th Century."* http://www.kennesaw.edu/hss/wwork/domesticity/mh/bloomers_cc.htm (accessed on September 3, 2012).

Brassiere

A garment made to cover, contain, and support women's breasts, the brassiere has long been identified with femininity, female sexuality, and even female oppression. Originally thought to have been invented during the early 1900s, when women were beginning to gain some independence, the brassiere, or bra, represented freedom from much more restrictive undergarments, such as tight corsets, a tightly fastened body suit designed to push up or flatten a woman's breasts or to hug her waist until her figure assumed an "hourglass" shape. By the second half of the century, the bra itself had come to represent restriction and many women rebelled against wearing it.

While it has been long thought that the brassiere was a twentieth-century invention, archeological research by the University of Innsbruck begun in 2008 and publicly announced in 2012 revealed evidence of brassieres being worn by women more than six hundred years ago. Four bras from a castle in Austria were found largely intact, and radiocarbon dating traced the garments to the fifteenth century. The bras were very much like the modern version, with shoulder straps and cups, and possibly a back strap as well. In addition, the research revealed that far from being solely utilitarian, these undergarments were seen as ornamental lingerie meant to please both the wearer and her suitor, an assumption derived from the intricate lace ornamentation on the items.

As the era of the stiff corset came to an end in the late nineteenth century, fashion designers, along with women themselves, began to seek alternative undergarments. In 1914 a young New York socialite named Polly Jacob (she later used the name Caresse Crosby) tied two handkerchiefs together with ribbon to make the first brassiere of the modern era. She eventually sold the right to make the new garment to Warner Brothers Corset Company. At almost the same time in France, designer Paul Poiret (1879–1944) created a similar garment. These early bras were designed to flatten the breasts, since small breasts were fashionable at the time. By the end of the decade another New Yorker, Ida Cohen Rosenthal (1886–1973), had designed a new, more fitted brassiere, with cups. She started the Maidenform Company to manufacture and sell the new bra.

A larger bustline was popular during the 1930s, and designers introduced an "uplift" bra, with padding and extra reinforcement to help women maximize their figures. Padded bras became popular again during the 1950s, when big

A women modeling a half-slip and bra. The brassiere represented freedom to women accustomed to tight corsets.
© VINTAGE IMAGES/ARCHIVE PHOTOS/GETTY IMAGES.

breasts were in style again. The increasingly casual style of the 1960s led to a "braless" look. For those too timid to give up bras altogether, there were soft, stretchy bras that combined the braless look with a little support. Going braless became a form of political statement among many in the women's rights movement, as many feminists rebelled against society's rules about how women were supposed to dress. At the 1968 Miss America contest, feminists (supporters of equal rights and treatment for women) protested male beauty standards by throwing curlers, makeup, and bras into a garbage can. Although no bras were burned, the media exaggerated the event, and the term "bra-burner" became a generically pejorative synonym for "feminist."

The jogging craze of the late 1970s and early 1980s led many women back to bras for support. Two University of Vermont students, Hinda Miller and Lisa Lindahl, sewed two men's athletic supporters to elastic straps and created the first jogging bra. Soon jogging bras, or "sports bras," were designed so that they could be worn without a shirt. During the 1990s the exposure of cleavage, the depression between a woman's breasts, came back into style and another new type of bra was developed. Called the Wonderbra, this bra pushed the breasts up so that even small-breasted women could have a fashionable bustline.

SEE ALSO *Volume 3, Eighteenth Century: Corsets; Volume 5, 1980–99: Wonderbra*

For More Information

Dowling, Claudia Glenn. "Ooh-la-la! The Bra." *Lif*e (June 1989): 88–96.

Farrell-Beck, Jane. *Uplift: The Bra in America.* Philadelphia, PA: University of Pennsylvania Press, 2002.

Hawthorne, Rosemary, and Mary Want. *From Busk to Bra: A Survey of Women's Corsetry.* Cincinnati, OH: Seven Hills Book Distributors, 1987.

Jahn, George. "600-Year-Old Linen Bras Found in Austrian Castle." *Yahoo! News,* July 19, 2012. http://news.yahoo.com/600-old-linen-bras-found-austrian-castle-192408678.html (accessed on September 2, 2012).

Pasternak, Anna. "Fast Track to Femininity: Why Competing With Men Has Left Women Out of Touch with Their Feminine Side." *Daily Mail.* http://www.dailymail.co.uk/femail/article-1039030/Fast-track-femininity-Why-competing-men-left-women-touch-feminine-side.html (accessed on September 2, 2012).

Taylor, Kate. "Today's Ultimate Feminists Are the Chicks in Crop Tops." *Guardian,* March 23, 2006. http://www.guardian.co.uk/commentisfree/2006/mar/23/comment.gender (accessed on September 2, 2012).

Collars

Collars are neckbands attached to the neckline of a shirt. Removable collars were invented in 1827 by Hannah Montague (1794–1878) of Troy, New York. They fastened either at the front or the back of a shirt with a collar button, a stud on a shaft that slips through two small eyelets on a collar. They became popular money-saving items when clothing was custom-sewn and expensive. Collars detached from the body of shirts for laundering separately, which extended the life of the shirt. Even after shirts became mass manufactured, removable collars remained popular. They were a common part of men's, and some women's, wardrobes into the 1930s.

Montague's invention so impressed manufacturers in Troy that they began mass-producing detachable collars locally for sale to a world market. Making these collars called for only a small investment; factory workers, usually low-paid women, needed only scissors, material, and a spool of thread to cut and sew collars. So successful was the venture that Troy became known as "collar city," with twenty-five collar factories by 1897.

During the first two decades of the twentieth century, collars were manufactured primarily in white. They were made of cotton and linen fabrics and made stiff by dipping them in thin cooking starch. "Linene" collars were cotton bonded to thin but stiff cardboard called card stock, and "linex" collars were linen bonded to card stock. Others were bonded to celluloid, a flammable substance mainly used in the manufacture of movie film. Straight-standing collars for formal wear were worn with evening suits. These collars were very rigid and ranged in height from 2 to 3 inches (5 to 8 centimeters). A sudden jerking of the head could cause a chafing at the bottom of the jaw with these collars. For less formal functions, a man wore a "wing" collar, a hard collar with the front edges folded downward to resemble wings, or a "fold-over" collar, a hard collar that is turned down. A collar might cost thirty-five cents individually, or four to five dollars for a box of twenty-five collars.

For business and leisure wear, various styles of white detachable collars were worn with pastel or bright-colored shirts in solids, patterns, or stripes. As office work became more widespread in the early 1900s, the prestige attached to a clean white collar led to the term "white-collar worker," a term that is still in use to refer to office or business professionals. Women who chose to wear tailored suits with shirtwaists and ties also sometimes wore detachable collars.

During World War I (1914–18), soldiers in the United States armed forces wore soft-collared uniforms. After the war men's styles became more relaxed for the comfort of the wearer. Detachable "spread" collars, extended flat collars, as opposed to straight-standing, made of softer materials became popular. By the 1930s only older, conservative dressers kept the tradition of detachable collars.

For More Information

Keers, Paul. *A Gentleman's Wardrobe: Classic Clothes and the Modern Man*. New York: Harmony Books, 1987.

Peterson, Amy T. *The Greenwood Encyclopedia of Clothing Through American History 1900 to the Present*. Westport, CT: Greenwood Publishing Group, 2008.

Shep, R. L., and Gail Cariou. *Shirts & Men's Haberdashery*. Mendocino, CA: R. L. Shep Publications, 1999.

Turbin, Carole. "Fashioning the American Man: The Arrow Collar Man, 1907–1931." *Gender and History* 14, no. 3 (November 2002): 470–91.

Driving Clothes

Driving, or motoring as it was known in the early years of the twentieth century, inspired its own fashion trend, born out of the need to protect automobile drivers and their passengers from the elements. The short-lived craze for driving clothes that emerged in the first decade of the twentieth century also reflected a trend toward the development of specialized garments for special occasions.

Driving clothes were more than stylish clothing to complement the earliest cars; they also were very practical. The earliest cars gave motorists no protection from the weather. Rain, wind, and cold air threatened to soak or chill motorists, and open cars traveling at high speeds over unpaved country roads covered drivers with dust. Both men and women welcomed the protective driving clothes introduced between 1900 and 1910.

For men, the outfit started with a cloth peaked cap and a set of driving goggles that could be pushed up onto the forehead when not in use. On warm, dry days, a driving coat, or duster, completely protected the wearer's suit from dust. Dusters were typically made of cotton, silk, or linen and colored gray to conceal the accumulated dust. If the weather became more severe, a leather, fur, or fur-lined topcoat, or stormcoat, could be substituted. An 1899 edition of the *London Tailor* recommended "loose coats of goatskin and loose pantaloons of the same,

Driving clothes were stylish as well as practical, helping protect driving enthusiasts from rain, snow, and dirt. © STOCK MONTAGE/ARCHIVE PHOTOS/GETTY IMAGES.

gloves, and snow boots" for winter driving and a "long hooded great coat with deep collar and a yachting cap" for summertime.

Women also wore long protective coats, though they tended to prefer specially designed face veils to goggles. These large, usually gray veils could be tied around the fashionable hats of the day and adjusted to cover the entire head, protecting the wearer not only from dust but also from oil stains and other unpleasant hazards. Some women motorists also tried hoods that could be fastened under the chin or adopted men's peaked caps or woolen tam-o'-shanters, flat caps with a tight headband and floppy large crown topped with a pompon. Still others wore large face-covering bonnets, like beekeepers' hats, with a glass window to see through, or carried tiny hand-windshields, which they held in front of their faces to keep dust and bugs out of their eyes.

Some elements of driving clothes have survived into the modern day, but generally they represent a specific niche market. These include items like driving shoes, made to be very flexible and with soles that adhere better to the accelerator, brake, and clutch pedals than conventional shoes, and soft, leather driving gloves, designed to be stylish but also to protect the hands from calluses and give a better grip on the steering wheel. White, cotton driving gloves are still popular among both male and female professional drivers (bus and taxi drivers) in Asia and can be purchased in automotive supply stores. In Japan, a minimum standard of dress is required in order for prospective drivers to take their practical driving test. Clothing or footwear seen as inappropriate—such as sandals—are disallowed. Candidates who do not pass the standard are turned away and told to return on another date and wear more appropriate attire for driving.

For More Information

"Classic Car Clothing, Period Motoring Clothing." *Greycar.com*. http://www. greycar.com/ (accessed on September 2, 2012).

"Mens Driving Shoes." *Mens Fashion Authority*. http://www.mens-fashion-authority.com/mens-driving-shoes.html (accessed on September 2, 2012).

Perry, Amy. "Why Mens Driving Gloves Are Making a Big Comeback." *Market Press Release,* December 14, 2011. http://www.marketpressrelease.com/Why-Mens-Driving-Gloves-Are-Making-a-Big-Comeback-1323900534.html (accessed on September 2, 2012).

Russell, Douglas A. *Costume History and Style.* Englewood Cliffs, NJ: Prentice-Hall, 1983.

Yarwood, Doreen. *The Encyclopedia of World Costume.* New York: Charles Scribner's Sons, 1978.

Hobble Skirts

During the first decade of the 1900s, just as women began demanding more freedom, more rights, and more comfortable fashions, one of the most restrictive styles of the nineteenth and twentieth centuries came into style. This was the hobble skirt, a tight, ankle-length skirt that grew narrower at the hem. Popular between 1905 and 1910, the hobble skirt was so tight at the ankles that the woman wearing it could only walk in very short steps.

In the early 1900s many westerners were fascinated by the clothing styles of Asia and the Middle East. Famous French fashion designer Paul Poiret (1879–1944) created many popular designs based on Eastern clothing. The hobble skirt, which reached its peak of popularity in 1910, was a variation on the harem skirt designed by Poiret to resemble the styles of the Middle East. Another popular variation on the same design was the peg skirt. Like the hobble skirt, the peg skirt was tight at the hem, but it was wider at the top, creating a loose blousy effect as the skirt tapered sharply in at the bottom. Both of these types of the skirts forced the wearer to walk with tiny steps, the way many westerners imagined women might walk in the East.

Horses are hobbled by tying their front legs together with a short rope to prevent them from running away. The hobble skirt was named after this practice. Women who wore the skirt often wore another type of hobble as well. The hobble garter was a band made of fabric that was worn under the hobble skirt, wrapped around each leg just below the knee. A band connected the legs, preventing the wearer from accidentally taking too long a step and ripping her fashionable hobble skirt. Some hobble skirts also were made with a slit in the back to make walking easier. When sitting, the slit could be buttoned in order to keep the ankles modestly covered.

The popularity of the restrictive hobble skirt did not last long, as women continued to press for more freedom in their lives and their

A Western woman wearing a hobble skirt, with its traditional tapering towards the bottom.
© GENERAL PHOTOGRAPHIC AGENCY/STRINGER/HULTON ARCHIVE/GETTY IMAGES.

clothing. By the 1920s women's fashions had become much less confining. The hobble skirt wearer, shuffling along with tiny steps, was replaced by the flapper, dancing a wild Charleston in a loose skirt that was hemmed up to the knee.

Although hobble skirts as everyday women's wear have long been abandoned, the fashion lives on well into the twenty-first century. Hobble skirts have become a popular item among fetish fashion enthusiasts. The restrictive qualities of the skirt have become a selling feature for some, and hobble skirts made from such materials as leather and PVC are the most prominent and may even include unique features like padlocks in order to prevent the wearer from easily removing the item.

For More Information

Baudot, François. *Poiret*. Translated by Caroline Beamish. London, England: Thames and Hudson, 1997.

Bels, Annebeth. "Pride Feels No Pain, Nor a Hobble Skirt." *The Mere Alchemist*, November 28, 2011. http://themerealchemist.blogspot.jp/2011_11_01_archive.html (accessed on September 3, 2012).

"Chanel Revives the Hobble Skirt at Haute Couture Show." *Her World Plus*. http://www.herworldplus.com/shopping/updates/shopping-updates-chanel-revives-hobble-skirt-haute-couture-show (accessed on September 3, 2012).

Hoobler, Dorothy, and Thomas Hoobler. *Vanity Rules: A History of American Fashion and Beauty*. Brookfield, CT: Twenty-First Century Books, 2000.

Mackrell, Alice. *Paul Poiret*. New York: Holmes & Meier, 1990.

Miller, Brandon Marie. *Dressed for the Occasion: What Americans Wore, 1620–1970*. Minneapolis, MN: Lerner Publications, 1999.

Hunting Outfit

Hunting in the early years of the twentieth century combined two activities for which specialized clothes were developed: riding horses and shooting. Until the second half of the nineteenth century, men had hunted in a version of their normal attire. That changed with the introduction of the sack coat and the lounge jacket, both of which were adapted for riding with the addition of vents to allow freedom of movement. By the turn of the century a wing-shape cut had evolved, along with special riding jackets accompanied by flared skirts and vents. In addition, riding breeches had largely replaced trousers by the 1890s.

When shooting, the typical English huntsman of the first decade of the twentieth century wore a tweed jacket with or without leather gun pads at the shoulders. The most popular type of hunting jacket, in England as well as in the United States, was the Norfolk jacket. The Norfolk was modeled after the hunting suit worn on the estate of the Duke of Norfolk in the early nineteenth century. Tradition has it that the Prince of Wales himself ordered a garment from his tailors that would allow him to swing a gun with greater ease than the tight-fitting, tailored suit jackets he usually wore. The jacket's pockets were large enough to hold small game, or animals. The Norfolk jacket was unusual in two ways: as the rare garment that was specifically designed rather than adapted for use in sports; and as a waist-length jacket that did not require matching trousers.

To complete his outfit, the early twentieth-century hunter wore cloth breeches or knickerbockers (short pants that fasten tightly at the knee), stockings, and boots. Beginning in the first decade of the twentieth century, black jack-boots (heavy riding boots with high plain tops) were popular, though after a couple of seasons a novice hunter could expect to graduate to top boots (black boots with brown leather tops). On the head, felt or tweed caps and hats were common, including the tweed "fore-and-aft," or deerstalker cap, with its earflaps tied over the top of the head. Silk top hats and bowler hats also were quite fashionable while hunting.

An informal variation on hunting attire also developed during this period. Called the "ratcatcher" after a remark by King Edward VII (1841–1910) to one of his lords, the style combined riding jacket, cloth breeches, and a cloth cap or soft felt hat. Ratcatcher hunting attire is still worn in certain seasons or under certain conditions in both the United States and Great Britain into the twenty-first century.

Hunting clothes allowed for the freedom of movement necessary for the hunt. © SZ PHOTO/SCHERL/DIZ MUENCHEN GMBH SUEDDEUTSCHE ZEITUNG PHOTO/ALAMY.

For More Information

Contini, Mila. *Fashion: From Ancient Egypt to the Present Day*. Edited by James Laver. New York: Odyssey Press, 1965.

Cosgrave, Bronwyn. *The Complete History of Costume and Fashion: From Ancient Egypt to the Present Day*. New York: Checkmark Books, 2000.

Kybalová, Ludmila, Olga Herbenová, and Milena Lamarová. *The Pictorial Encyclopedia of Fashion*. Translated by Claudia Rosoux. London, England: Paul Hamlyn, 1968.

Wilton, Mary Margaret Stanley Egerton, Countess of, and R. L. Shep. *The Book of Costume: Or Annals of Fashion (1846) by a Lady of Rank*. Lopez Island, WA: R. L. Shep, 1986.

Jumper Gown

Jumper gowns were popular during the first few years of the twentieth century. They were long skirts with 2- to 3-inch-wide (5- to 8-centimeter wide) attached suspenders, or straps extending over the shoulders from the front waist to the back waist, also known as bretelles. Jumper gowns were worn over blouses or guimpes, yokes or collars of fabric that look like the upper part of blouses and that cover the neck and shoulders. They also were worn over lingerie shirtwaists, undergarments resembling tailored blouses that were meant to be worn under guimpes.

In 1908 jumper gowns were highly fashionable among American women. They were designed to emphasize a slim waist and full hips. They featured heavy flared, pleated skirts made up of four or more panels. The suspenders were cut in one piece of fabric extended from the skirt and joined at the shoulders by straps of velvet ribbon. Some skirts had as many as nine panels of fabric and were so long the hemlines dropped below the ankles and touched the floor. Hemlines might measure as much as 5 yards (5 meters) of fabric at the bottom. Jumper gowns of this sort were worn by wealthy women who had dressmakers sew them in silk, taffeta, satin, or linen fabrics. Depending upon the fabrics and the trims, jumper gowns could serve as dress-up outfits or casual wear for leisure activities.

Affordably priced McCall's sewing patterns made it possible for women of lower economic circumstances to sew their own jumper gowns. Unlike the affluent women, working women and less well-to-do housewives created jumpers from fabrics made from wool and cotton. The less expensive jumper gowns were rarely made up of more than four panels of fabric, and most of the hemlines hung an inch (3 centimeters) above the floor in order to avoid fraying the fabric. In place of ribbon trims, less costly jumpers occasionally were fastened at the shoulders by buttons. While guimpes for the wealthy were made of lace, silk, or lavish embroidery, and their blouses were made of silk or satin, less expensive guimpes and blouses primarily were sewn in cotton.

During the 1910s women's styles became less burdensome and more relaxed. As women spent more time walking and taking part in work and leisure activities, they chose hemlines that no longer touched the floor. Also, as loose, flexible undergarments replaced rigid, boned corsets, jumpers evolved into one-piece, loose-fitted sleeveless ankle-length dresses under which shirtwaists or blouses were worn.

For More Information

Ewing, Elizabeth. *History of Twentieth Century Fashion*. Revised by Alice Mackrell. Lanham, MD: Barnes and Noble Books, 1992.

Waugh, Norah. *The Cut of Women's Clothes, 1600–1930*. New York: Theatre Arts Books, 1994.

Knickers

Popular among late nineteenth-century English country gentlemen, early twentieth-century sportsmen, and young American boys of both centuries, knickers are short pants that are characterized by a band that fastens tightly at the knee, similar to the breeches of the fifteenth through eighteenth centuries. (As a clarifying point, the term "knickers" is also used in modern British English to refer to women's underwear, or what American English would call "panties," and care should be taken that the terms are not confused.)

Usually made of a sturdy fabric like wool or corduroy, knickers have been dressed up with jackets to form knicker suits, and dressed down as the playing uniform for early baseball players. Though they are still worn occasionally into the twenty-first century as an artistic fashion statement or chic sportswear, knickers disappeared from everyday fashion during the 1930s.

From the fifteenth through the eighteenth centuries, knee breeches or pants were common, daily wear for men. They were replaced during the 1800s by long trousers, which then became the standard accepted male attire. However, many men found that when working or playing sports outside, the new long pants became wet and dirty, especially in wet climates, like that of Great Britain. Many of these men chose to wear

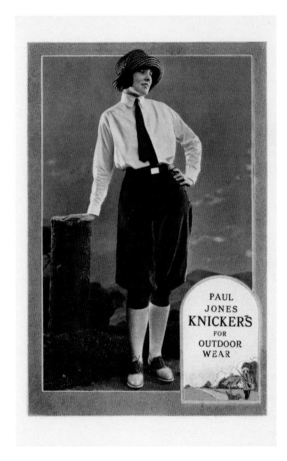

Though knickers were most often associated with young boys, men and even some women wore the knee-length pants. © LCDM/UNIVERSAL IMAGES GROUP (LAKE COUNTY DISCOVERY MUSEUM)/ALAMY.

a kind of knee pants with a band that fastened just above the knee. To cover the leg below the knee, they wore long woolen socks or leather or canvas leg wraps called puttees. Though the earliest versions of these short pants closed just below the knee, by the early 1900s they usually fastened just above the knee.

One group of men who wore this style of trousers was the Dutch immigrants who settled in the state of New York during the 1600s. These New York Dutch were given the name "Knickerbockers," which was a variation of the name of a prominent Dutch family. Soon their distinctive knee pants were called knickerbockers as well, and the name was commonly shortened to knickers. In the mid-1800s one of the first baseball teams formed in New York. They called themselves the Knickerbockers, and the stylish and practical knickers were part of their uniform.

Though many men and even some women wore knickers for work or sporting activities at the turn of the century, by the 1910s they were most commonly identified with small boys' clothing, especially in the United States. While toddlers of both sexes were usually dressed in skirts, young American boys of four and five began to wear the knee-length knickers with long knee socks. The transition from knickers to long pants was seen as a milestone, when a boy became a man.

SEE ALSO *Volume 3, Sixteenth Century: Hose and Breeches; Volume 3, Seventeenth Century: Breeches; Volume 3, Eighteenth Century: Knee Breeches*

For More Information

Laver, James. *Costume and Fashion: A Concise History.* 4th ed. London, England: Thames and Hudson, 2002.

Men's Fashion Illustrations from the Turn of the Century. New York: Dover Publications, 1990.

Yarwood, Doreen. *The Encyclopedia of World Costume.* New York: Charles Scribner's Sons, 1978.

Peg-Top Clothing

The great fashion shift of 1908 brought important changes to both men's and women's silhouettes, the outline of the body that is the basic form of a new style. One of the most important changes was the introduction of a tapered look from the hips to the ankles. Before 1908, for example, the silhouette for women called for an S-shape, with protruding breasts and buttocks, and bulky, flowing skirts. After 1908 the silhouette became much more natural, with clothes staying closer to the actual shape of the body. But the clothing of this period was not altogether natural: pegging, or creating width in the hips and closeness at the hem, introduced a look that was very popular from 1908 up to the beginning of World War I in 1914.

Men had worn peg-top trousers off and on since trousers became more widespread beginning in the nineteenth century. These trousers had an abundance of material at the hips, which gave a baggy look. Pleats and panels allowed the trouser legs to narrow dramatically to a close-fitting hem at the ankle. These styles came back into fashion for men, adding a rare spark to the rather dull men's clothing of the time. When women went into factories in great numbers during the war they often wore peg-top trousers, which fit a woman's shape better than straight trousers and added a stylish touch to otherwise drab outfits.

The peg-top look was most striking with women's clothes, and it was used with both skirts and suits. The peg-top look could be subtle, with soft billows at the hips narrowing to a close-fitting but not restrictive hemline. But the peg-top look that got the most attention was anything but subtle. Large pleats and carefully tailored panels could make the skirts balloon outward at the hips, giving the appearance of large saddlebags, or covered pockets, and then taper severely to a tight ankle. When worn with a close-fitting jacket as part of a peg-top suit, the look was quite dramatic.

Peg-top clothing for women marked a real break from older styles, but it hardly gave women freedom to move with ease. In 1912 a tailor providing guidance on sewing such a skirt warned that if a woman in a peg-top suit found herself in an emergency the only way she could move quickly was to hop like a kangaroo. Like the hobble skirt, which it resembled, peg-top skirts and suits went out of style by 1914. Pegging, or restricting the width of a hem, returned at various points in the century as a way of changing the shape of garments.

Fashion, Costume and Culture, 2nd edition   **671**

SEE ALSO *Volume 4, 1900–18: Hobble Skirts*

For More Information

Batchelor, Bob. *American Popular Culture Through History: The 1900s*. Westport, CT: Greenwood Publishing Group, 1992.

Payne, Blanche, Geitel Winakor, and Jane Farrell-Beck. *The History of Costume*. 2nd ed. New York: HarperCollins, 1992.

Sack Suit

The men's suit had been evolving ever since the seventeenth century, when men first began wearing a coat over a shirt and vest. By the end of the nineteenth century the basic suit had reached the form that we know today, with trousers, sleeveless vest, and coat made from the same material. While suits could take many forms, including the dressy tuxedo with tails and the self-indulgent lounge suit, a loose-fitting suit with longer tails on the jacket, the least formal and most often worn suit was the sack suit. Simple in cut and conservative in style, the sack suit, or three-piece suit, has been the basic suit of the Western businessman for more than one hundred years.

The sack suit was very simple, and it did retain its basic form throughout the twentieth century, but this does not mean that it didn't go through a variety of subtle changes as men sought ways to keep up with fashions. In the first years of the twentieth century the coat was buttoned high on the chest, fastened with four buttons, and had a very small collar and lapels (folds on the front of the coats). After about 1910, however, sack suit coats more commonly had three buttons and larger collar and lapels. The neckline dropped and stayed at mid-chest for the rest of the century. Suit coat pockets, typically appearing at the hip line, could either have a simple slit opening or a flap.

Trousers often showed variation in their fit and detailing. The presence or absence of cuffs and the appearance and sharpness of creases and pleats were both areas where fashion made its influence felt. The most dramatic changes came in the fit of the trousers. In the early 1900s trousers were loosely fitted, but the peg-top craze of 1908 through 1914 saw men's trousers get baggy in the hips and very slim at the ankles. After World War I (1914–18) trouser styles straightened out once again. Men could show their personal sense of style most easily with the vest. Vests might be worn in contrasting colors and patterns, with silk piping at the edges and pockets, or with fancy collars.

Men's sack suits were a kind of uniform for men in business, but wealthy or fashion conscious men could make a statement with their suits. They might go to an expensive tailor to have their suit carefully fitted, or they might add stylish details or accessories like a beautiful silk tie or a handkerchief carefully folded into the front pocket. Men's suits became very stylish in the 1930s and 1940s, and in the 1980s men chose expensive suits from well-known designers, called power suits, to display their status.

In modern men's fashion, suits are available in a variety of styles, although one of the most prominent features is the number of buttons the suit features. Generally ranging between one and four buttons, and sometimes even more, styles change from year to year, with many men's fashion magazines, such as *GQ,* ready to guide consumers to the most current trends. While the two-button suit has been a standard in the world of business, one-, three-, and even four-button suits have been seen worn by famous politicians, businessmen, and entertainers.

SEE ALSO *Volume 3, Nineteenth Century: Ditto Suits; Volume 4, 1930–45: Men's Suits; Volume 5, 1980–99: Armani Suits*

For More Information

"Best Suit for the Office." *GQ,* August 2003. http://www.gq.com/style/style-guy/suiting/200308/two-three-four-button (accessed on September 3, 2012).

Keers, Paul. *A Gentleman's Wardrobe: Classic Clothes and the Modern Man.* New York: Harmony Books, 1987.

Payne, Blanche, Geitel Winakor, and Jane Farrell-Beck. *The History of Costume.* 2nd ed. New York: HarperCollins, 1992.

Schoeffler, O. E., and William Gale. *Esquire's Encyclopedia of 20th Century Men's Fashions.* New York: McGraw-Hill, 1973.

"Tips to Choose Between 1 Button or 3 Button Suit." *Men's Italy.* http://www.mensitaly.com/mens_one_button_suits/mens_1_button_suits.htm (accessed on September 3, 2012).

Shirtwaist
• •

The shirtwaist was a tailored blouse or shirt worn mainly by working-class women in the early years of the twentieth century. The shirtwaist was often worn with a fitted or looser A-line long skirt. Sometimes it was

The Gibson Girl

First appearing in published illustrations in the late 1800s, the Gibson girl was the creation of American artist Charles Dana Gibson (1867–1944). Gibson's art depicted the fashionable upper-middle-class society of his time, particularly a certain type of modern young woman. Independent, athletic, and confident, the Gibson girl was also pretty and feminine, illustrating some of the contradictions of modern womanhood at the turn of the twentieth century. The Gibson girl was important for several reasons. She depicted the modern woman, known popularly as the "new woman," at a time when more women gained independence, began to work outside the home, and sought the right to vote and other rights. The Gibson girl had a real influence on the fashions of the time, as the illustrations were widely published and imitated from around 1890 until 1910.

As the 1900s began, society was changing rapidly. The Industrial Revolution of the nineteenth century made manufactured goods more widely available and created more jobs. While poor women had always worked, more and more middle-class women began to work outside the home. By 1900 more than 5 million women in the United States had jobs, and by 1910 the number had risen to 7.5 million. These women needed fashions that would enable them to be more active. Between 1890 and 1910 styles became simpler and more practical. Skirts were long and flared, and dresses were tailored with high necks and close-fitting sleeves. The style was considered masculine, and this was sometimes emphasized by wearing a necktie. Though women still wore the restrictive undergarments known as corsets, a new health corset came into style that was said to be better for the spine than earlier corsets. An S-shaped figure became trendy, with a large bust and large hips, separated by a tiny, corseted waist. These styles, worn with confidence and poise by modern women, caught the eye of artist Charles Dana Gibson.

Gibson was born in Roxbury, Massachusetts. He trained as an artist and met some success selling his drawings while he was still a teenager. Gibson made a specialty of drawing society scenes. He was very observant, and his drawings always contained humor and insight

worn with a "tailor-made," which was a skirt-and-jacket suit. The shirtwaist had a rounded neck or came with a tailored collar. Many buttoned up the back, and women who could not reach behind them had to call upon a husband or female family member to close the tiny buttons.

The advantages of wearing shirtwaists were many. Shirtwaists emphasized a natural waistline to give a flattering look to the figure. They allowed freedom of movement. The garments were manufactured in volume and therefore were affordable. They were relatively small items and could be washed by hand in a sink or washbowl and ironed quickly.

Even though many women wore corsets underneath shirtwaists to maintain sculptured figures, the shirtwaist was a liberating item of about the world around him. *Life* magazine published much of Gibson's work. During the 1890s he used his wife, Irene Langhorne, as a model for a series of drawings of modern young women at work and at play, in all the latest, less-restrictive fashions. The Gibson girl was tall, athletic, and dignified. She might be pictured at a desk in a tailored shirtwaist or at a tennis party in an informal sports dress. She wore her long hair upswept in an elaborate mass of curls, perhaps topped by a simple straw hat. Though she was capable and independent, the Gibson girl was always beautiful and elegant.

Though the Gibson girl was American, she was soon widely imitated both in the United States and abroad. Women across all classes in society wanted to wear the fashions they saw in Gibson's drawings. Even men imitated the look of the broad-shouldered, mustached Gibson man who often accompanied the women in Gibson's work. The popularity of the Gibson look spread quickly, thanks to new national magazines that reached large numbers of readers. Newly developed businesses, such as Sears and Roebuck's mail order catalog and clothing pattern catalogs, also helped make it easier than ever for the average woman to gain access to the latest fashions.

The S-shaped silhouette of the Gibson girl was widely imitated. © AMERICAN STOCK ARCHIVE/ARCHIVE PHOTOS/GETTY IMAGES.

clothing. It took the place of the stiff, tight, high-collared bodices of the nineteenth century.

By the early 1910s cotton shirtwaists were worn by hundreds of thousands of working women. Through the decade the garment changed according to fashion trends. Early shirtwaists featured pleats in the shoulders that reflected the puffy-shouldered Gibson girl look popularized in the sketches of American artist and fashion illustrator Charles Dana Gibson (1867–1944). By 1914 shirtwaists had less rigid puff shoulders and often were worn untucked so that some fabric flowed below the natural waist. That look later made way for the dropped-waist dresses of the 1920s.

Women wearing shirtwaists with long flowing skirts.
© DAZO VINTAGE STOCK PHOTOS/IMAGES.COM/ALAMY.

Shirtwaists worn by housewives and female factory workers usually were solid white cotton blouses with simple pleating that allowed for mobility. Shirtwaists also served as garments of female office workers, or even as dressier fare. Better quality daytime shirtwaists were made of fine cotton, silk, or linen. Fancier shirtwaists could be part of evening outfits. These more decorative garments often were custom sewn. They featured such fabrics as silk, laces, taffeta, and sateen and some displayed lively patterns.

Because the shirtwaist was primarily a working woman's blouse, it most commonly was manufactured as ready-to-wear clothing. One of the factories that produced this item was the Triangle Shirtwaist Factory in New York City. In 1911 this factory entered history books as a place of infamy when it burned down. Lacking any safety codes to protect workers, the disaster resulted in the deaths of 146 female workers. The disaster led to a major upgrade in safety regulations for factory workers.

For More Information

Ballentine, Michael. "Those Glorious Gibson Girls." *Town and Country* (May 1983): 194–204.

Gibson, Charles Dana, and H. C. Pitz. *The Gibson Girl and Her America.* New York: Dover, 1969.

Kheel Center, Cornell University Library. *The Triangle Factory Fire.* http://www.ilr.cornell.edu/trianglefire (accessed on September 3, 2012).

Lieurance, Suzanne. *The Triangle Shirtwaist Fire and Sweatshop Reform in American History.* Berkeley Heights, NJ: Enslow, 2003.

Snyder-Haug, Diane. *Antique & Vintage Clothing: A Guide to Dating and Valuation of Women's Clothing, 1850–1940.* Paducah, KY: Collector Books, 1997.

Trench Coats

The long, water-repellent coat known as a trench coat was adapted from military use and became enormously popular during and after World War I (1914–18). Stylish and functional, the trench coat, traditionally made of a rugged fabric called gabardine, remained a staple of outerwear throughout the twentieth century and was adopted by some of the most notorious, as well as the most revered, figures in history and popular entertainment.

The cloth from which trench coats are made dates from the 1870s, when British clothier Thomas Burberry (1835–1926) developed a unique wool material that was chemically processed to repel rain. Burberry succeeded in creating a fabric that was tear-resistant, virtually crease-proof, and resistant to the elements, while remaining porous and well-ventilated enough to be comfortable and cool for the wearer. Burberry called his innovative fabric gabardine, and it transformed modern rainwear. Jackets made of the fabric were first used in the Boer War fought in South Africa between the British and Dutch settlers from 1899 to 1902, and it was called a Burberry.

The outbreak of World War I in 1914 created a need for a bad-weather garment to protect the soldiers fighting in the trenches (long pits dug into the ground for defense). Burberry designed a coat made of fine twill gabardine that repelled water while allowing the wearer

Originally developed for the British military, the trench coat was introduced for civilian use after World War I and has remained popular ever since. © JAMES JENKINS - VISUAL ARTS/ALAMY.

freedom of movement. Dubbed the trench coat or storm coat, it quickly became the official coat of the Allied fighting man, someone who fought Germany and its allies during World War I. It is estimated that half a million Burberry trench coats were worn by combat officers between 1914 and 1918. Aquascutum Limited, another prestigious firm in London, England, also turned out trench coats for the British military. At the war's end, the trench coat was introduced for civilian use, becoming the world's most famous and enduring weatherproof style.

The classic World War I-era trench coat was double-breasted, with four buttons, reinforced shoulder or gun flaps, straps at its sleeves, a buckled all-around belt (with distinctive brass "D" rings designed to hold one's water bottle, hand grenades, or sword), slotted pockets, and an adaptable collar. It was typically lined with wool. While these features have been altered somewhat over the years, the trench coat has never gone out of fashion, remaining a popular all-purpose coat with both men and women. Among its wearers are a number of famous political leaders, actors, and literary figures, including politicians Winston Churchill (1874–1965) and Ronald Reagan (1911–2004), actors Humphrey Bogart (1899–1957) and Katharine Hepburn (1907–2003), writer George Bernard Shaw (1856–1950), and General Norman Schwarzkopf (1934–). Fictional characters who have become identified with the trench coat include Holly Golightly, the heroine of the novel and film *Breakfast at Tiffany's* (1961), and Peter Sellers' bumbling Inspector Clouseau from the *Pink Panther* comedy film series.

Trench coats also have been associated with some of the most infamous villains of history, both real and fictional. Around the time of World War II, trench coats worn with fedora hats became a signature garment for the Nazi German secret police, the Gestapo. One of Hitler's generals, Alfred Jodl, also wore a black leather trench coat, an image many times reproduced in films about the war. Trench coats have also been featured in fictionalized and historical images of 1920s Chicago mobsters like Al Capone.

For More Information

Chenoune, Farid. *A History of Men's Fashion*. Paris, France: Flammarion, 1993.

Foulkes, Nick. *The Trench Book*. New York: Assouline, 2007.

Keers, Paul. *A Gentleman's Wardrobe: Classic Clothes and the Modern Man*. New York: Harmony Books, 1987.

Schoeffler, O. E., and William Gale. *Esquire's Encyclopedia of 20th Century Men's Fashions*. New York: McGraw-Hill, 1973.

Underwear for Men

At the turn of the twentieth century many men wore union suits as undergarments. Union suits were one-piece, knit undergarments that covered both the upper and lower body. The traditional union suit was made of cotton or wool and covered the body from the ankles to the wrists. It had a long row of buttons up the front and featured a buttoned drop seat in the rear. Union suits often shrunk when washed, making the garments uncomfortable. They also were bulky and tended to irritate the wearer. Despite these problems, they were practical undergarments that provided warmth before the days of central heating.

During the first few years of the century, several factors influenced the shape and the style of men's underwear. First, the widespread use of central heating meant that men no longer needed to wear long underwear indoors. Secondly, men's fashions began to be fitted more closely to the body, making bulky undergarments impractical. Thirdly, as sports and athletics became more popular as leisure activities, men sought out lighter forms of underwear. To accommodate these changes, underwear factories such as Chalmers Knitting Mills in Amsterdam, New York, began manufacturing less bulky, mesh garments that were comfortable for summer weather. By 1911 the first newspaper advertisements promoted patented, or original, advances in men's underwear styles. They included improvements in crotch closures and seat flaps, allowing for more comfort and better hygiene.

The athletic union suit was introduced in the early 1910s. It was a knee-length one-piece garment with a sleeveless top that gave men more mobility. In 1912 Chalmers advertised a cotton-knit athletic union suit called the Porosknit, which featured a sturdy cotton yoke front. This model boasted a no-bulge waistline and easy-to-fasten buttons that did not easily come undone; it was also breathable, which meant that air flowed easily through the fabric, keeping the wearer from getting too hot.

During World War I (1914–18) several changes occurred in the shape and styling of men's underwear. Men started wearing two-piece undergarments. The bottoms, often referred to as drawers, were knee-length cotton shorts with a few front buttons for durability and comfort. Certain models laced up at the side. Most drawers were made of cotton, although wealthy men wore silk drawers. On the upper body men wore chemises, sleeveless tops that covered the upper torso and tucked into the drawers.

Men's underwear followed this basic pattern into the twenty-first century, with both tops and bottoms made in a variety of styles. For the bottoms, men can choose from longer, looser boxer shorts, close-fitting but modest briefs, or skimpy, skin-tight bikini underwear. For the tops, men typically choose from either V-necked or crewneck T-shirts or tank tops.

For More Information

Cunnington, C. Willett, and Phyllis Cunnington. *The History of Underclothes*. New York: Gordon Press, 1979.

Schoeffler, O. E., and William Gale. *Esquire's Encyclopedia of 20th Century Men's Fashions*. New York: McGraw-Hill, 1973.

Waugh, Norah. *Corsets and Crinolines*. New York: Theatre Arts Books, 1970.

Zippers

Zippers are devices for fastening clothing. A zipper consists of two tracks of teeth or coils, made of metal or synthetic plastic materials, which are connected to a pull-piece that either locks or separates the tracks.

The "automatic continuous clothing closure," an early form of a zipper, was patented in 1851 by American inventor Elias Howe (1819–1867), who also invented the sewing machine. Howe never marketed his form of the zipper. More than forty years later Chicago-based engineer Whitcomb L. Judson (c. 1846–1909) designed and patented another early form of a zipper, a series of hooks and eyes, or holes, that came together mechanically. Judson's fastener was used in closing mail pouches, tobacco sacks, and men's boots. Legend has it that Judson invented this "clasp locker" because he was a heavy man who had difficulty bending over to fasten the individual buttons or clasps on his own boots. With American businessman Colonel Lewis Walker (1855–1938), Judson marketed his invention through the Universal Fastener Company of

Chicago, Illinois, and called it the "Judson C-curity Fastener." Their product was displayed at the 1893 Chicago World's Fair but did not succeed commercially. The Judson invention failed to sell because it jammed easily and came undone accidentally. It also had to be removed from a garment before washing because it rusted when wet. The fastener was so complicated to use that it even came with an instruction booklet.

Early in the twentieth century Gideon Sundback (1880–1954), a Swedish immigrant to the United States who was an electrical engineer, was hired by the Universal Fastener Company. His job as head designer was to improve the Judson invention in order to make it more marketable. By the end of 1913 Sundback had invented the modern zipper. It was made up of two rows of teeth that came together with a single slider. Sundback also designed a machine to manufacture his fasteners. During World War I (1914–18) the United States government purchased the Sundback fasteners for use on items ranging from large pouches to military uniform trousers to aviator, or pilot, clothing. After the war the fasteners were used on raincoats, overalls, swimming trunks, and tennis racquet covers. In 1923 the B. F. Goodrich Company of Akron, Ohio, bought the Sundback invention for use on its line of rubber boots. They named their product "the Zipper Boot" after the sound the slider made as it skated along the metal tracks. The name stuck, and zippers became one of the most common clothing fasteners of modern times.

The world's largest zipper manufacturer for many decades has been the Japanese company, Yoshida Kogyo Kabushiki Kaisha (or Yoshida Manufacturing Corporation). Its iconic "YKK" initials are emblazoned on the majority of the world's zippers. By the 1960s, YKK had 95 percent of the zipper market share, and the company continues to produce in excess of 7.2 billion zippers worldwide annually, earning 4.3 billion dollars in profits by the early years of the twenty-first century. In 2011 YKK Group's revenues were 7 billion dollars.

The zipper is one of the most common clothing fasteners, found on everything from boots to jackets to jeans. © DJA65/ SHUTTERSTOCK.COM.

For More Information

Friedel, Robert. *Zipper: An Exploration of Novelty*. New York: W. W. Norton, 1994.

Fulford, Benjamin. "Zipping Up the World." *Forbes,* November 24, 2003. http://www.forbes.com/global/2003/1124/089.html (accessed on September 3, 2012).

Walker, Lewis. *The Lengthened Shadow of a Man*. New York: Newcomen Society of North America, 1955.

YKK Corporation. "YKK Annual Report." March 2011. http://www.ykk.com/english/corporate/financial/annual/index.html (accessed on September 3, 2012).

Headwear, 1900–18

During the first years of the twentieth century, women continued to wear their hair and hats much as they did in the previous century, but after about 1908 styles began to change and the first of the styles that would become so popular during the 1920s and 1930s appeared. In terms of hair and hats, this was an age of transition.

Hair historian Richard Corson claims in *Fashions in Hair: The First Five Thousand Years* that "the first half of the twentieth century was, perhaps, the least colourful period in history for men's hair styles." Men wore their hair short as a rule, and the widespread use of pomades, or oily hair dressings, tamed even the most naturally curly hair into standard styles, parted on the side or in the middle. It became the custom in the twentieth century for men to visit barbershops regularly to receive a haircut and a shave. Barbershops were a common feature of American towns, but they also were very popular in France, where men could get their hair cut cheaply. Beards and mustaches went out of style in this period and were generally worn only by older men. The mark of the modern man was to be clean-shaven. Though their hairstyles may have been bland, men brought real variety to their wardrobe by choosing from amongst a wide variety of hats, from derbies to fedoras and Panama hats to top hats.

At the beginning of the twentieth century women wore their hair much as they did in the previous century: very long, then braided and piled into elaborate hairdos that were topped with richly decorated hats. The key to women's hairstyles was size, with hair reaching both high and

Irene Castle

One of the most famous and successful performers of her time, Irene Castle (1893–1969) was a creative ballroom dancer and a tremendous influence on American and European fashions of the 1910s. Along with her husband and dance partner, Vernon (1887–1918), the elegant Irene brought respectability and social acceptance to dozens of new modern dances. At the same time, the Castles' dancing enlivened respectable society with the exciting new rhythms of ragtime music and dance. The public also admired Irene Castle for her tall athletic figure and her modern sense of style. Women everywhere imitated her short hair and loose clothing, and many fashion historians consider Castle the first flapper.

Born in New Rochelle, New York, in 1893, Irene Foote was drawn to the theater from early childhood. She took dancing lessons and performed in a few local productions, but her dream of a career onstage did not come true until 1910, when she met a British dancer and comic named Vernon Castle. Castle had already begun a career in vaudeville, a variety stage

show popular from the early 1890s to the mid-1920s. Within a year the pair were married, and they soon began performing a dance show in Paris, France, at the popular nightclub Café de Paris. They were an immediate hit and soon began dancing professionally at society clubs and parties all over Europe.

The early 1900s had seen a tremendous rise in the popularity of an energetic, jazzy music called ragtime, which was influenced by the rhythms of African American music. As ragtime became more popular, many new dances were introduced to go with the new music. Between 1912 and 1914 more than one hundred new dances were introduced. These new dances were seen as sexy and wild, and while many modern young people loved them, older, more conservative people found them shocking. Irene and Vernon Castle created toned-down versions of these wild modern dances. Together the Castles created many of their own dances, such as the "Castle Walk," the "Castle Lame Duck Waltz," and the "Castle Half and Half." They helped bring the dance craze to respectable

wide. To achieve the coveted size women draped their hair over pads or wire frameworks, or they used false hairpieces. Some women spent hours working their hair into the desired styles. Hairstyles did grow smaller and less elaborate after 1910, and entertainer Irene Castle (1893–1969) introduced the first short hairstyle for women in 1913, the precursor to the bobbed styles of the 1920s.

Modern hair care products had still not been invented, so most women cared for their hair with homemade shampoos and treatments. A beauty manual published in 1901, for example, recommended washing the hair once every two weeks with a shampoo made from eggs and water. Women used petroleum jelly, castor oil, and other sticky substances to society. In 1914 they brought their dance show to the United States and were soon making five thousand dollars per week, at a time when the average worker made about fifteen dollars per week.

Irene's influence reached far beyond dancing. Tall, slim, and tomboyish, she became one of the most imitated women of her time. When she cut her hair short, women across the United States went to hairdressers demanding the "Castle crop." For ease in dancing, Irene stopped wearing a corset and adopted straight loose dresses, and women began to throw away their corsets. The pearl headband she frequently wore over her hair became the popular "Castle band," and a perky feathered hat she wore became the "Castle hat." The flapper look of the 1920s began with the Castle look of the 1910s.

World War I began in 1914, and in 1916 Vernon Castle went back to England to join the air force. He was killed in a plane crash in 1918, and the Castles' influential dance partnership ended. Irene tried to maintain her dance career with other dance partners but was never again as successful or as famous. She remarried three times before she died in 1969.

Irene Castle, dancing with husband Vernon, was one of the most famous fashion trendsetters of her time.
© EVERETT COLLECTION INC./ALAMY.

soften their hair and hold it in place. The introduction of the permanent wave process in 1906 allowed women to curl their hair, though the process was costly and time consuming. The first hair dryer was introduced about the same time, though it wasn't perfected until the 1920s.

Hats were an essential part of every woman's wardrobe, and the size and variety of hats available during this period are nothing less than astonishing. Hats were big in the first years of the century and, contrary to the simplifying trend in women's dress that occurred after 1908, they grew bigger and more ornate over time. From the Gainsborough chapeau to the *Merry Widow* hat, women's headwear during this period represented the pinnacle of the headdresser's art.

For More Information

Amphlett, Hilda. *Hats: A History of Fashion in Headwear.* New York: Dover, 2003.

Castle, Irene. *Castles in the Air.* New York: Doubleday, 1958.

Corson, Richard. *Fashions in Hair: The First Five Thousand Years.* London, England: Peter Owen, 2001.

Ewing, Elizabeth. *History of Twentieth Century Fashion.* Revised by Alice Mackrell. Lanham, MD: Barnes and Noble Books, 1992.

Payne, Blanche, Geitel Winakor, and Jane Farrell-Beck. *The History of Costume.* 2nd ed. New York: HarperCollins, 1992.

Trasko, Mary. *Daring Do's: A History of Extraordinary Hair.* New York: Flammarion, 1994.

Barbershops

The traditional American barbershop was an emporium where men congregated to have their hair cut, faces shaved, and fingernails manicured. Barbershops, particularly those in small towns, also served a wider purpose within the community. They were places where men gathered, relaxed, read magazines, and enjoyed each other's company while passing gossip, sharing the latest joke, talking sports and politics, and debating the events of the day.

For many centuries a man's hair was trimmed at home, usually by a servant or a family member. Shaving before the invention of the razor blade was a messy and sometimes painful affair. All this began to change in the United States in the mid-nineteenth century, first with the increasing number of small towns sprouting up across the country and, later on, with the evolution of the razor blade. In the early twentieth century shaving and short hairstyles became fashionable, and a barbershop could be found on the main street of just about every small town and all over the major cities.

The traditional barbershop was distinguished from other businesses by the red and white or red, white, and blue-striped pole that stood out front. In the seventeenth century, barbers rather than medical doctors performed surgeries, due to the fact that the Catholic Church prohibited doctors (who were mostly educated at church-owned universities) from doing so. In England, these barber-surgeons adopted the use of red and white striped poles outside their places of business. The red and white were historic symbols of the blood-soaked rags and bandages; the blue was added to make the pole resemble the American flag. On the inside the barbershop was outfitted with the supplies that were necessary for a barber to practice his trade: razors; strops, or strips of leather or horse-hide, for sharpening blades; shaving bowls and mugs; hair combs and brushes; soap; scissors; mirrors; popular hair tonics; barber's chairs; talcum powder; and towel steamers.

The men in barbershops occasionally sang together for their amusement, a trend that gave rise to the barbershop quartet. These musical groups performed the types of songs that were popular between the 1860s and the 1920s: tunes featuring innocent, sentimental lyrics and simple melodies that were easily harmonized. By the early 1900s the term "barbershop" was commonly used to indicate singing. An early written reference is a barbershop-style song, "Play That Barbershop Chord," published in 1910.

Around the turn of the century, the typical price for a haircut and a shave was twenty-five cents, or "two bits." So steeped in American culture was the ubiquitous barbershop that the phrase "shave and a haircut, two bits" entered the vernacular and was transformed into a musical couplet used at the end of many bluegrass songs. Transcending its bluegrass origins, even to this day the unmistakable riff can be heard either as a melody or tapped out as a rhythm, like a secret doorknock. It was even used by American prisoners of war (POW) in Vietnam as a code to identify each other. A former POW, Ernest C. Brace, told the story of how he met Senator John McCain. McCain knocked out the first five beats of the "shave and a haircut" rhythm on the wooden wall of the enclosure where they were kept. Brace, a new prisoner, was on the other side of the wall, and while he couldn't see McCain, being American he instinctively tapped back the last two beats, "two bits," in response.

For decades men visited the barbershop for their daily shave; however, the evolution of the electric and the safety razor and the increasingly hectic pace of modern life combined to make shaving at home a more practical pursuit. The traditional barbershop fell out of favor in the 1960s as young men began wearing their hair longer. Another factor that helped kill off the tradition was the widespread prohibition on barbers using straight razors for shaving customers. Fueled by public health concerns over blood-borne illnesses like hepatitis and HIV, many states and regions put strict regulations on what was seen as a risky practice. In the twenty-first century, laws on barbershop shaving vary widely from state to state and country to country. However, the traditional barbershop had been largely replaced by the modern, unisex hair salon, although barbershops still exist across the United States.

For More Information

Adams, Cecil. "What's the Origin of the Barber Pole?" *The Straight Dope*, December 28, 2000. http://www.straightdope.com/columns/read/1868/whats-the-origin-of-the-barber-pole (accessed on September 3, 2012).

Barlow, Ronald S. *The Vanishing American Barbershop.* El Cajon, CA: Windmill Publishing Company, 1993.

Brace, Ernest C. "Messages from John." *Wall Street Journal,* May 2, 2008. http://web.archive.org/web/20081201165511/http://www.johnmccain.com//Informing/News/NewsReleases/3168f3a2-e59b-433f-94ea-fb1641323507.htm (accessed on September 3, 2012).

Hunter, Mic. *The Vanishing American Barbershop: A Closer Look at a Disappearing Place.* Mount Horeb, WI: Face to Face Books, 1996.

Staten, Vince. *Do Bald Men Get Half-Price Haircuts?: In Search of America's Great Barbershops.* New York: Simon and Schuster, 2001.

Men's Hats

In the first decades of the twentieth century there were so many different kinds of hats that a man could truly wear a hat for nearly every occasion. And, if he wanted to be considered a gentleman, he absolutely could not go without a hat. The cultural traditions favoring headwear for members of both sexes were very strong. Hat wearing would eventually go out of style by the second half of the century, but in the years between 1900 and roughly 1950, hats were an essential part of a man's wardrobe.

Headwear came in two basic styles: the hat and the cap. Caps were made of a soft fabric, usually wool and wool tweed but sometimes another fabric, and were generally brimless and sat close on the crown of the head. Caps were generally favored for more vigorous outdoor activities and for motoring, or driving a car. More common and far dressier than the cap was the hat, made of a heavy and almost always stiff material such as felt or straw, with a distinct brim and a crown that stood away from the top of the head. Hats came in a variety of styles, with the primary differences coming in the size and shape of the brim and crown, the material, and the color.

The most popular hat in the years up through World War I (1914–18) was the derby, called the bowler in England. Usually made of black or brown felt, with a round crown of moderate height and brim that was curled up all the way around, the derby could be worn for nearly

Until the mid-twentieth century, hats were an essential part of every man's wardrobe. © VINTAGE IMAGES/ALAMY.

every occasion but the most formal. Two other felt hats, the homburg and the fedora, also were very popular, multipurpose hats. The homburg was fairly formal, with a slightly curled brim and an indent running the length of the crown. The fedora was a flamboyant hat, with multiple indents in the crown and brim that could be snapped up or down, giving it the nickname "snap-brim."

The hat of choice for formal occasions was the top hat, a flat-brimmed hat made of black silk, with a taller, straight-edged crown. Top hats were often worn with a hatband, a narrow band of fabric in a contrasting color that sat at the base of the crown. Another specialized hat was the Panama hat, a wide-brimmed, stiff straw hat with a high crown typically worn only in the summer. A variation on the Panama hat was the sailor hat, which had a low, flat cylindrical crown and a 2-inch (5-centimeter) or wider brim. With the vast number of hats available, many of them in a range of colors, men could always find a hat to match their outfit and the occasion.

SEE ALSO *Volume 3, Nineteenth Century: Top Hat; Volume 4, 1919–29: Derby; Volume 4, 1919–29: Fedora*

For More Information

Bigelow, Marybelle S. *Fashion in History: Apparel in the Western World.* Minneapolis, MN: Burgess Publishing, 1970.

Folledore, Giuliano. *Men's Hats.* Hollywood, CA: Quite Specific Media Group Limited, 1996.

Keers, Paul. *A Gentleman's Wardrobe: Classic Clothes and the Modern Man.* New York: Harmony Books, 1987.

Payne, Blanche, Geitel Winakor, and Jane Farrell-Beck. *The History of Costume.* 2nd ed. New York: HarperCollins, 1992.

Schoeffler, O. E., and William Gale. *Esquire's Encyclopedia of 20th Century Men's Fashions.* New York: McGraw-Hill, 1973.

Permanent Wave

During the late 1800s and early 1900s, several hairdressers discovered that by applying chemicals and heat to women's hair, they could create curls and waves that would last for days, weeks, or even months. These hairstyles were called permanent waves or simply permanents. Permanents brought the latest technology into the world of women's fashion and beauty, and, because the machines were located in shops, rather than the home, they made women's hair care into a social event rather than a private ritual.

A French hair stylist named Marcel Grateau (1852–1936) invented the first long-lasting hair waving technique in 1870. Grateau experimented with new ways of using a heated iron to curl hair until he came up with a method that created waves that remained in the hair for days. Modern women were eager to find ways to style their hair that took less time, and many began to have their hair "marcelled," as Grateau's process was called. In 1906 Charles Nestlé, a Swiss hairdresser working in London, England, invented a new and even more permanent way to style hair. His first permanent wave machine used gas to heat hair that had been wrapped around chemically treated pads. This actually caused the chemical composition of strands of straight hair to break down and re-form in curly strands, creating a wave that lasted for months. Later machines used electricity to heat the hair.

The early part of the 1900s was an exciting time of new inventions and new freedoms for women. People wanted to try modern ways of doing things, and they wanted the latest styles, in hair as well as in clothes.

Though the early permanent wave machines looked very strange, with separate wires leading to each chemical-wrapped curl, they were the most modern, and many women wanted to try the new style. New stores called beauty shops began to open, offering haircuts, styling, and permanent waves. These shops created places for women to gather and socialize while their hair was done.

While those women with straight hair wanted permanent curls and waves, others with naturally curly hair wanted their hair straightened. An African American hairdresser named Marjorie Joyner (1896–1994) invented a new, more compact permanent wave machine that also worked to straighten very curly hair. Patented in 1928, the machine was a dome-shaped helmet that used electrical current to heat hair which was clamped in 1-inch (3-centimeter) sections.

A woman with hair styled in a permanent wave. © W. W. CHERRY/HISTORICAL/CORBIS.

While the procedure and chemicals used have changed many times from the early days, permanents, or to use the more modern term, perms, continue to be popular in the twenty-first century. Both men and women continue to have their hair permed or straightened to appear fashionable and to keep up with the latest hairstyles.

For More Information

Corson, Richard. *Fashions in Hair: The First Five Thousand Years.* London, England: Peter Owen, 2001.

McCarthy, Laura Flynn. "The New Wave." *Vogue* (September 1989): 652–56.

Sherrow, Victoria. *Encyclopedia of Hair: A Cultural History.* Westport, CT: Greenwood Publishing Group, 2006.

Trasko, Mary. *Daring Do's: A History of Extraordinary Hair.* New York: Flammarion, 1994.

Women's Hats

Of all the items worn between 1900 and 1918, perhaps the most spectacular and varied were women's hats. Women's hats were large and heavily ornamented in the first half of this period, providing a good

Women at the beginning of the twentieth century wore large and heavily ornamented hats to complement their dresses. © EVERETT COLLECTION INC./ ALAMY.

match for women's dresses. When women's styles grew sleeker and more closely fitting after 1908, hats got even larger and carried even more ornament. No well-dressed woman appeared in public without a hat during this era, and fashionable women took great care to ensure that their hats were one-of-a-kind.

Women wore their hair very long in this period, and they then piled it atop their head in great mounds that provided a sturdy base for a hat. Hats were secured to the head with long hatpins stuck through the hat and into the mound of hair. According to fashion historian Elizabeth Ewing in *History of Twentieth Century Fashion,* these ornamented hatpins "had lethal projecting points which menaced anyone who approached the wearer too closely."

The more modest hats had a sturdy basic form made of felt or fabric, stiffened into shapes with brims and crowns of many different sizes. These hats could be ornamented with a feather or a giant ribbon, but they generally extended beyond the head no more than a few inches. More adventuresome women used hat frames that were made of wire, around and through which were woven long strips of lustrous fabrics, flowers, strips of lace, feather, ribbons, and other ornaments. A single hat frame could be modified to create all kinds of effects or to match a particular outfit. One of the most popular ornaments was an aigrette, a tall spiky feather from an egret.

The most spectacular hats began to appear around 1908. As women's dresses got smaller, hats got bigger. One of the most popular hats was the nineteenth-century Gainsborough chapeau, a very wide-brimmed hat that sat high on a pile of hair. The round brim of a Gainsborough chapeau could extend beyond a woman's shoulders, and the addition of large puffs of ribbon or ostrich feathers might make the hat as tall as it was wide.

These large hats posed a problem for increasingly active women. Their great size made any quick movement very difficult, so they required many hatpins and hooks to secure them in place. As more and more people began to travel in automobiles, most of which had open tops, milliners developed special hat coverings, or veils, to protect hats and hair from wind and dust. These motor veils were usually large mesh veils that were secured around the neck and covered most of the head. Some motor veils had just a hole for the eyes, and a few covered the entire head and face.

Perhaps the most famous hat of the period was the *Merry Widow* hat, created in 1907 by Lady Duff-Gordon (1863–1935; Lucy Christiana Sutherland), an English designer, for the play of the same name. Three feet (one meter) wide and eighteen inches (forty-six centimeters) tall, the hat was liberally mounded with ribbon and feathers. Stylish women rushed to copy the style, but theater-goers in London, England, complained so loudly that such hats were blocking their view that this and other huge hats were banned from theaters. By the end of World War I (1914–18) such large hats had disappeared from the public eye altogether.

Although large, extravagant hats have long been abandoned as common fashion accessories for women, there are occasional exceptions to the rule, such as the annual Kentucky Derby horse race at Churchill Downs in Louisville, Kentucky. For this event, the tradition of dressing up and wearing ornate hats continues, more than a century after the first running of the race. Almost like a costume ball, women compete to wear some of the most outlandish, outrageous creations, many of which are reminiscent of the hats worn at the turn of the twentieth century. Veils, feathers, ribbons, flowers, extremely wide brims, loud colors, and all types of hats from the elegant to the gaudy are in ample supply and worn by celebrities and ordinary visitors alike.

SEE ALSO *Volume 3, Nineteenth Century: Gainsborough Chapeau*

For More Information

Bigelow, Marybelle S. *Fashion in History: Apparel in the Western World.* Minneapolis, MN: Burgess Publishing, 1970.

Cummings, Darron. "138th Kentucky Derby Hats." *Los Angeles Times,* May 5, 2012. http://www.latimes.com/features/image/la-138th-kentucky-derby-hats-20120505,0,6661721.photogallery (accessed on September 3, 2012).

Ewing, Elizabeth. *History of Twentieth Century Fashion.* Revised by Alice Mackrell. Lanham, MD: Barnes and Noble Books, 1992.

Payne, Blanche, Geitel Winakor, and Jane Farrell-Beck. *The History of Costume.* 2nd ed. New York: HarperCollins, 1992.

Body Decorations, 1900–18

In an age of extravagant dresses and immense feathered hats for women, and conservative suits and carefully chosen hats for men, body decorations and accessories faded in significance. It wasn't that such items were not important to people in the early years of the twentieth century; rather, they were simply overshadowed by the showiness of other parts of the outfit, as in the case of women, or were very understated, as in the case of men.

Women were certainly highly ornamented, especially in the first decade of the twentieth century. Their exquisitely tailored long dresses were topped off by closely fitting collars that accented the length of the neck, and their hats were among the most extravagant items ever to be worn. After about 1908, when skirts lifted to reveal the feet and ankles, shoes also became a way to show off one's fashion sense. Accessories, however, were downplayed. Most women carried a purse or small handbag, and the beaded purse, with its great versatility, was among the favorites. For evening wear a woman might slip on long gloves that extended as high as the elbow, and for colder weather a fur muff kept the hands warm. Most women wore jewelry but it was typically rather understated. Smaller earrings, rings, and a necklace of pearls were considered quite tasteful. Women also might carry a watch on a gold chain.

Women's makeup began to go through major changes around the turn of the century. Most women continued to use their own homemade makeup to lighten their faces or add color to their lips or cheeks. But modern manufacturers and distributors soon offered help. The precursor

Madame C. J. Walker

The first woman in the United States to become a millionaire through her own work, Madame C. J. Walker (1867–1919) was a pioneer in the creation of cosmetics created specifically for black women. An African American woman herself, Walker not only invented many products for black women's hair and skin, but, in the early 1900s, she also created a very successful business based on door-to-door sales of her products. Madame C. J. Walker cosmetics paved the way for later door-to-door cosmetics companies, such as Avon and Mary Kay. Walker was not only a successful businesswoman, she was also a leader in the black community and a lifelong supporter of women's economic independence.

Walker was born Sarah Breedlove in Delta, Louisiana, just after the end of the American Civil War (1861–65). Her parents were farmers who had been slaves for most of their lives, and Sarah's early life was full of poverty and hard work. Her parents died when she was seven, she was married at fourteen, and she was widowed by the age of twenty. In 1905 she moved to Denver, Colorado, where she married a reporter named C. J. Walker. Though they divorced in 1912, Madame Walker used his name for the rest of her life. Along with working as a laundress and a cook, she began to sell cosmetic products door-to-door for a company started by another African American woman, Annie Malone (1869–1957). By this time she noticed that her hair was falling out, which was not uncommon for black women, who often had stressful lives and poor nutrition caused by poverty. Walker was determined to find a

to the Avon cosmetics company was founded in the United States in 1886 and by 1906 had more than ten thousand representatives offering a line of 117 different products to women across the country. Madame C. J. Walker (1867–1919) invented a line of cosmetics for African American women in the same decade. Modern advertising made many more women aware of the "need" to wear cosmetics, driving the sale and use of such items to new levels among women of all social classes.

Men's costume in general was quite conservative during this period, which meant that accessories provided men with some small element of personal expression. Several items were popular among men. Many men carried pocket watches on a chain, and the quality and style of the chain was a mark of distinction. Men might also carry a walking stick, and these sticks could be decorated with a carved gold or wooden handle, or have a decorative metal tip. Finally, the most distinctive items of male jewelry were all forms of fasteners: cuff links to hold shirt cuffs together; a stickpin to hold the tie in place; or studs and buttons to fasten the shirt. Such small items, when made in fine gold, could signal the wearer's wealth and taste.

solution to the problem, both for herself and for thousands of other African American women.

Some stories of Walker's life say that she had an aunt who knew how to use healing herbs. Others say she had a dream in which a black man gave her the formula for a hair tonic. However it happened, Walker took $1.50 she had saved from her laundry work and began to make and sell her own hair product, "Madame Walker's Wonderful Hair Grower." She traveled throughout the U.S. South, selling her products and building her business. By 1910 Walker had opened a factory in Indianapolis, Indiana, to make the many beauty products she developed with African American women in mind. She also hired hundreds of women, most of them African American, to sell her products door-to-door. In 1908 she opened a school for "hair culturists" who would sell and teach women how to use Madame Walker's products.

Walker contributed a great deal to the cosmetics industry, which was just beginning during the early part of the twentieth century. Her products and sales techniques were original and were a model for many companies that followed her. African American women were often forgotten by white businesses, but they too wanted to take part in the glamorous, more liberated fashions of the turn of the century. Walker not only offered a wide variety of products for women who had had very few beauty products before, she also offered jobs and financial independence to many black women. At the time of her death in New York in 1919, the Madame C. J. Walker Manufacturing Company was earning $250,000 per year and employed more than ten thousand women. The company survived until 1985, when it was sold by her heirs.

For More Information

Avon Products, Inc. "Experience Avon's History." *Avon.com: The Company for Women.* http://www.avoncompany.com/aboutavon/history/index.html (accessed on September 3, 2003).

Bundles, A'Lelia. *On Her Own Ground: The Life and Times of Madam C. J. Walker.* New York: Scribner, 2001.

Lowry, Beverly. *Biography of Madame C. J. Walker.* New York: Knopf, 1999.

Payne, Blanche, Geitel Winakor, and Jane Farrell-Beck. *The History of Costume.* 2nd ed. New York: HarperCollins, 1992.

Peacock, John. *Fashion since 1900.* London: Thames and Hudson, 2007.

Beaded Handbags

Women have been carrying purses or small handbags since the Middle Ages (c. 500–c. 1500). Though the first purses were simple leather pouches covered with a flap, women soon developed purses and handbags into decorative accessories that could be matched to their outfits and adorned with all manner of ornament. From 1900 to 1918 one of

the more popular styles was the beaded handbag. This small bag, about the size of a grapefruit or smaller, was made of fabric that was covered in small beads. The opening was secured either with a metal clasp or a snap. The handbag might have a long chain or cord, but many had no strap at all and were simply held in the hand.

The real artistry in a beaded handbag came in the design of the beadwork. Designs could be very simple, with opalescent beads of a single color or just slightly contrasting colors, or they could be very complex, with many different colors arranged into dramatic patterns. Beaded handbags remain a popular accessory to this day.

For More Information

"Fashion Is in the Bag: A History of Handbags." *RandomHistory.com.* http://www.randomhistory.com/2008/10/01_handbag.html (accessed on September 11, 2012).

Grafton, Carol Belanger. *Shoes, Hats, and Fashion Accessories: A Pictorial Archive, 1850–1940.* Mineola, NY: Dover Publications, 1998.

Payne, Blanche, Geitel Winakor, and Jane Farrell-Beck. *The History of Costume.* 2nd ed. New York: HarperCollins, 1992.

Although created in the early twentieth century, the beaded handbag remains a popular accessory to this day. © DEA/A. DAGLI ORTI/DE AGOSTINI PICTURE LIBRARY/GETTY IMAGES.

Lipstick

Cosmetic products intended to color the lips have been used for thousands of years, by both women and men, in a variety of shades, depending on the fashion of the time. Modern lipstick, consisting of waxes, oils, and pigments pressed into a cylinder and packaged in a metal tube, has been sold to women since 1915. Some women feel almost undressed without their lip coloring, and industry experts estimate that the average twenty-first century woman uses between 4 and 9 (2 and 4 kilograms) pounds of lipstick in her lifetime.

Social customs in the West had discouraged the use of cosmetics for several hundred years, but that began to change around the turn of the twentieth century. As women began to hold jobs and demand the right to vote and other privileges afforded only men, their lives became less restricted. Cosmetics such as rouge, powder, and lipstick came into style, and such respectable companies as the Sears and Roebuck Catalog began to sell them. In the early 1900s women like Helena Rubenstein (1870–1965), Elizabeth Arden (1884–1966), and Estee Lauder (1908–2004) went into the cosmetics business and began to sell cosmetics in their salons. Madame C. J. Walker (1867–1919) and Annie Malone (1869–1957) developed lipstick colors especially for African American women and sold them door-to-door.

During the flamboyant 1920s, dark red lipstick came into fashion, as women wanted to highlight their sexuality. Lipstick was packaged in small tubes, and for the first time women began to take it with them in a purse wherever they went. Glamorous dark lipstick hues continued to be popular throughout the 1930s. Maksymilian Faktorowicz, a Polish immigrant to the United States who changed his name to Max Factor (1877–1938), became a Hollywood makeup artist producing his own line of fashionable lipsticks. Factor also invented lip gloss, a clear lipstick that made the lips look shiny and moist. Many products, like lipstick, were unavailable during World War II (1939–45), but by the 1950s a glamorous look was in fashion once more. In 1949 a chemist named Hazel Bishop (1906–1998) invented "kiss-proof" lipstick that would not wipe off easily.

Lipstick shades vary as styles change. During the 1950s dark colors were fashionable, with Revlon's Fire and Ice being one of the most popular. Even white lipstick was popular for a short time during the 1960s, but soon a more natural look came into fashion. Today lipsticks can be found in a huge range of colors.

For More Information

Pallingston, Jessica. *A Celebration of the World's Favorite Cosmetic: Lipstick*. New York: St. Martin's Press, 1999.

Ragas, Meg Cohen, and Karen Kozlowski. *Read My Lips: A Cultural History of Lipstick*. San Francisco, CA: Chronicle Press, 1998.

Watches

A watch is a portable timepiece, most commonly carried in a pocket or strapped on the wrist. Pocket watches can be as large as 3 inches (8 centimeters) in diameter, while wristwatches are smaller, so that they do not interfere with the wearer's movement. Though they are usually worn for practical reasons, so that the wearer can keep track of the time, watches also are pieces of jewelry, which express the wearer's wealth, social status, and sense of style. Watches have become not only treasured family heirlooms, passed from one generation to the next, but also gifts to mark special times in a person's life, such as graduation or retirement.

The idea of the timepieces as an accessory is quite ancient. Romans as early as 500 B.C.E. carried small sundials as jewelry. The mechanical clock was invented in Europe around 1300 C.E., and portable miniature clocks soon followed. By the fifteenth century pocket timepieces became common accessories for both men and women. During the nineteenth century most those men who could afford to carry pocket watches did so. These watches were often gold or silver, with decorative covers that closed over the face. The most fashionable way to wear such a watch was tucked into a vest pocket, with a long gold chain that draped across the front of the vest to tuck in a buttonhole, often with a gold penknife on the other end. Working men sometimes carried their watches in a pants pocket in order to keep them from getting damaged. Women, on the other hand, wore their watches in a variety of fashionable ways. Some suspended a watch from a long chain around the neck, while others had a small watch attached to earrings or pinned by a ribbon at the waist.

Evidence of a watch attached to a bracelet comes from as early as the sixteenth century, but the first regular use came during the Boer War

Though used to keep track of the time, watches also reflect the wearer's wealth and sense of style. © GTS/SHUTTERSTOCK. COM.

between Great Britain and Dutch settlers in South Africa from 1899 to 1902. British officers needed to coordinate their attacks, and they didn't want to have to dig in their pocket for a watch. The wristwatch was the answer. The vast military movements of World War I (1914–18) required even better timing, and soldiers on both sides of the conflict began wearing self-winding wristwatches, which meant that they wound the watch with a small spindle on the side of the watch. Unreliable at first, they soon were made quite accurate. Men returning from the war kept their watches, and they became popular accessories. Soon, wristwatches were made with decorative leather or metal straps and with rich casings of gold, silver, or other precious metals. Wristwatches have been the most common form of timepiece ever since, both for men and women, and are available today in every price range, from a five-dollar plastic watch to a thirty-thousand-dollar gold Rolex.

Part of the importance of watches, especially in North America and Europe, has been due to the development of railways that connect distant cities and crisscross continents. Although the development of railways in Canada and the United States was a nineteenth-century development, by the turn of the twentieth century it became clear that highly accurate timepieces were critical for the smooth, safe operation of the railroads. In 1891 a horrific crash in Ohio that killed six postal clerks and two engineers happened when an engineer's watch malfunctioned. The accident led to a strict set of inspection standards and criteria for the manufacture of extremely accurate timepieces, known as railroad chronometers. Noted watch inspector Webb C. Ball created this set of rigid standards, which was later adopted by the Swiss Society of Chronometry (established in 1924) and became the foundation of a global standard of accuracy in timekeeping.

For More Information

Beitler, Stu. "Kipton, OH Train Collision, Apr 1891." *GenDisasters*, October 26, 2008. http://www3.gendisasters.com/ohio/9694/kipton-oh-train-collision-apr-1891 (accessed on September 3, 2012).

Dale, Rodney. *Timekeeping*. New York: Oxford University Press, 1992.

Edwards, Frank. *Wristwatches: A Connoisseur's Guide*. Willowdale, Canada: Firefly Books, 1997.

Tabler, Dave. "Making the Trains Run on Time." *Appalachian History: Stories, Quotes and Anecdotes,* January 14, 2009. http://www.appalachianhistory.net/2009/01/making-trains-run-on-time.html (accessed on September 3, 2012).

Terrisse, Sophie Ann, ed. *Prestigious Watches*. New York: St. Martin's Press, 1997.

Footwear, 1900–18

Men and women both enjoyed access to a wide range of footwear in the first decades of the twentieth century. In the last half of the nineteenth century several important breakthroughs had made shoes more comfortable and cheaper than ever before. The comfort came from the invention of shoes designed to fit right and left feet specifically. Up until this invention most people had worn straights, or shoes with straight soles that could be worn on either foot. Only the very rich could afford to have shoes custom made to their feet. Several different Americans invented machines to increase the speed of shoe production, especially the difficult job of sewing the uppers to the thick soles of shoes, and the first rubber heel for shoes was invented in 1899 by Humphrey O'Sullivan. Soon the United States led the world in shoe production. From heavy boots to dressy leather boots, and from comfortable tennis shoes to light sandals, people now had a great variety of shoes from which to choose.

Closely fitted high-top leather boots were one of the most popular shoe styles for both men and women at the turn of the century, and women especially liked these dressy boots as their skirt lengths became shorter and shoes became visible. By far the most popular shoe for women, however, was the pump. A pump was a moderately high-heeled shoe, usually made of leather, with an upper that covered the toes and wrapped around the side of the foot and behind the heel, leaving the top of the foot bare. These snug-fitting shoes were infinitely adaptable and could be made in any number of colors and decorated with buckles, ribbons, or other ornaments. Women who liked to dance preferred pumps with straps across the top to keep the shoe on. The pump remained one of the basic staples of dress shoes for women throughout the century.

While men in the nineteenth century had generally worn high-top shoes and boots, men in the first decades of the new century showed a distinct preference for low-cut shoes. The most popular shoe of the period was the oxford, which took its name from England's Oxford University, where the shoe originated. Made of leather or suede, the oxford slipped over the foot and was laced across the instep. Two-toned oxfords first became popular as summer wear in about 1912. Women also wore a variation of the men's oxford.

The tennis shoe, the most popular shoe of the twentieth century, got its start in the late nineteenth century but truly rose to prominence following the invention of the Converse All-Star basketball shoe in 1917. With a light canvas upper and rubber soles that grip the ground, these athletic shoes quickly became a favorite leisure shoe.

For More Information

Lawlor, Laurie. *Where Will This Shoe Take You?: A Walk Through the History of Footwear*. New York: Walker and Co., 1996.

Payne, Blanche, Geitel Winakor, and Jane Farrell-Beck. *The History of Costume*. 2nd ed. New York: HarperCollins, 1992.

Pratt, Lucy, and Linda Woolley. *Shoes*. London, England: V&A Publications, 1999.

Yue, Charlotte and David. *Shoes: Their History in Words and Picture*. New York: Houghton Mifflin, 1997.

Converse All-Stars

Converse paved the way for the athletic shoe explosion of the late twentieth century with its introduction of the canvas and rubber All-Star in 1917. It also created an enduring American footwear icon that still claims the allegiance of millions of wearers worldwide.

Marquis M. Converse founded the rubber footwear company that bears his name in 1908. The Converse brand grew briskly in the decade leading up to World War I (1914–18). But it achieved its greatest success following the introduction of the world's first basketball shoe in 1917. Dubbed the All-Star, the high top, black-and-white sneaker was distinguished by eight aluminum porthole eyelets running up each side and a bulbous toe made out of vulcanized rubber. The lightweight shoe provided excellent traction on the gymnasium floor for those playing the increasingly popular sport of basketball, invented by James Naismith (1861–1939) in 1891.

Helping to spur sales of the Converse All-Star was basketball player Charles H. "Chuck" Taylor (1901–1969), a sports legend from Indiana who joined the company's sales force in 1921. Taylor suggested a number of improvements for the shoe, including better ankle support and a sturdier sole. He also became one of the first well-known athletes to endorse a product. Taylor's input proved so effective that his signature was added to the sneaker's ankle patch in 1923. The shoes became informally known as "Chuck Taylors" or simply "Chucks" in his honor.

For many years Taylor worked tirelessly to promote the brand that bore his name. He drove around the United States with a trunkload of the canvas shoes, selling them to coaches and athletes at high schools and colleges. His work paid off. By the 1960s Converse dominated the basketball shoe market in the United States. Taylor himself was inducted into the Naismith Memorial Basketball Hall of Fame on the basis of his work on behalf of basketball footwear. Beginning in the late 1970s, however, Converse All-Stars fell out of fashion. First Adidas and Puma, then Nike and Reebok, began to attract young urban customers with new athletic shoe designs. In many instances these new brands successfully copied Converse's strategy by securing celebrity athlete endorsements for their products. Nike scored huge sales with its "Air Jordan," endorsed by basketball star Michael Jordan, for example.

In the late twentieth century the All-Star enjoyed a resurgence in popularity, thanks to its adoption by some rock stars and actors. Kurt Cobain (1967–1994) of the rock group Nirvana, for example, helped make Chuck Taylors an essential part of grunge fashion in the 1990s. The company was purchased by Nike in 2003.

Converse continues to operate as an independent subsidiary of Nike, producing and marketing its signature footwear products that bear the

Football players wearing Converse All-Stars, commonly called "Chucks." © BETTMANN/ CORBIS.

Converse name. The company produces the still-popular Chuck Taylor All-Star shoes in many different colors, and many special edition shoes have been made for purposes such as HIV/AIDS benefits or personalized designs for famous individuals or bands like AC/DC and Metallica. One recent company innovation was to allow customers to design their own Converse shoes, choosing from one of several basic models, and then customizing everything from cloth pattern to the colors of the laces and aluminum eyelets. In addition to their place in popular fashion, Converse shoes continue to be used by a number of professional athletes and teams in basketball.

For More Information

Converse. "About Converse." http://www.converse.com/About/ (accessed on September 3, 2012).

Jorgenson, Janice, ed. *Encyclopedia of Consumer Brands*. Detroit, MI: Gale, 1994.

Leibowitz, Ed. "Old Sneakers Never Die." *Smithsonian Magazine* (November 2001). http://www.smithsonianmag.com/people-places/Old_Sneakers_Never_Die.html (accessed on September 3, 2012).

Peterson, Hal. *Chucks!: The Phenomenon of Converse Chuck Taylor All Stars*. New York: Skyhorse Publishing, 2007.

High-Top Boots

Women's skirt lengths began to rise after about 1908, opening up a whole new world for the display of women's shoes. Skirt lengths did not rise much but just enough to display women's ankles and, perhaps, the lower length of the calf. For the woman who dared to wear the new higher skirts but was still modest, the high-top boot was the best choice of footwear. Stylish yet not revealing, it was one of the most popular shoes of the period.

The typical high boot was made of shiny black leather and laced up the center of the instep and to the top of the boot, which reached over the ankle and as much as several inches up the calf. Such boots always had a wide heel of perhaps 1 to 2 inches (3 to 5 centimeters) in height. Laces were the most popular method of securing the boot, but buttons were also quite common. The toes of these boots were alternately pointed or rounded, depending upon the current fashion.

High boots appeared in a broad range of styles and price ranges. One of the more common styles had the lower part of the boot made

The women on the right is wearing laced high-top boots, footwear that was considered stylish but not too revealing.
© SAZERAC, PARIS/VINTAGE IMAGES/ALAMY.

in one color of leather, usually black, with the ankle and calf covering made in a contrasting color, either in leather or fabric. Decorative elements like ruffles or lace might be added at the boot top, and stitching was common across the toe and the heel of the boot. While simple and inexpensive boots were available, wealthy women had boots made in fine kid leather, a soft leather made from the skin of a lamb or a goat, with delicate hand stitching.

Men's boots were quite similar to women's high boots, but in this period men more often chose to wear low shoes like oxfords.

For More Information

Grafton, Carol Belanger. *Shoes, Hats, and Fashion Accessories: A Pictorial Archive, 1850–1940*. Mineola, NY: Dover Publications, 1998.

Payne, Blanche, Geitel Winakor, and Jane Farrell-Beck. *The History of Costume.* 2nd ed. New York: HarperCollins, 1992.

Peterson, Amy T. and Ann T. Kellogg eds. *The Greenwood Encyclopedia of Clothing Through American History 1900 to Present.* Westport, CT: Greenwood Press, 2008.

Oxfords

Simply designed, low-cut shoes that lace up the front and have flat heels and thin soles, oxfords are the most common modern shoe for Western men. Many women wear them as well. Oxfords were worn in Europe as early as the 1640s, but they first became popular in Great Britain during the late 1800s and later throughout Europe and the United States. By about 1910 most men and boys wore lace-up oxford shoes for many social occasions.

During the 1800s both men and women wore boots or high-topped shoes that fastened with buttons. The lace-up oxford style shoe was originally a half boot worn by students at Britain's Oxford University, from which the style took its name. As the new shoe fashion spread at the beginning of the twentieth century, modern young people everywhere found oxfords attractive and comfortable. The new laces also made the shoe simpler to put on and take off than the older, time-consuming buttoned shoes. Though some men thought at first that the laces looked too feminine, they soon gave in and began wearing the new style.

The oxford style was flexible and could be used for dressy shoes as well as shoes for work and sport. Toes could be square or rounded, and some were decorated with stamped leather caps. These were called captoes or wing tips depending on the shape of the cap on the toe. Starting in the 1920s very fashionable young men wore two-toned oxfords, which used two different colors of leather in the same shoe to create a sporty look.

In the early 1900s women gained new freedoms. In many countries they were gaining the right to vote, as well as other rights, and a new image of the modern woman was emerging. This modern woman was more active and athletic, and her clothing was, therefore, both freer and sturdier. The new oxford style shoe fit this new active lifestyle perfectly. Although women did not wear them for formal occasions, they did wear oxfords for sports and other activities. Pioneer female aviator Amelia Earhart (1897–1937), who began her flying career during the early 1920s, was often pictured wearing oxford shoes.

SEE ALSO *Volume 4, 1919–29: Wing Tips*

For More Information

Schoeffler, O. E., and William Gale. *Esquire's Encyclopedia of 20th Century Men's Fashions.* New York: McGraw-Hill, 1973.

Yue, Charlotte, and David Yue. *Shoes: Their History in Words and Pictures.* Boston, MA: Houghton Mifflin Company, 1997.

Roaring Twenties: 1919–29

The ten years between 1919 and 1929 took Europeans and Americans on a social and economic roller-coaster ride. With the end of World War I in 1918, people abandoned their cautious attitudes caused by the uncertainty of war and embraced the freedom and joyousness of peace. Soldiers returned home to loved ones, and businesses shifted gears from supplying military needs to making commercial products. At the end of the war the United States was the strongest economy in the world. The country had supplied European and other nations with manufactured goods and agricultural products throughout the war, becoming a rich trader and source of investment dollars for the world. Britain, France, and especially Germany were devastated by the war. While Britain and France gradually recovered by mid-decade, Germany missed out on the prosperity enjoyed by other countries during the 1920s.

After a brief recession following the war, the U.S. economy began to prosper as never before. This success created new opportunities for most people, a larger middle class, and a higher standard of living. The economic boom gave more people money and created a strong demand for consumer products such as automobiles, radios, and household items. Cities swelled with skyscrapers housing new businesses, high-rise apartment buildings filled cities with prosperous people, and suburbs—or residential areas outside of cities—popped up around urban areas. These changes marked the 1920s as a time of optimism for most people. The decade came to be referred to as the Roaring Twenties to describe the newfound freedoms and sense of rebellion that people, who were often dressing in flashy and extravagant fashions, were experiencing.

Women want more

As the world shifted from focusing on the war to recreating normal domestic habits, however, the changes the war brought became very noticeable. Some things, people realized, would never be the same. When men

With more money in their pockets, people could afford to spend more on luxury items and tried to adopt more glamorous looks. © PLANET NEW ARCHIVE/SSPL/GETTY IMAGES.

had gone off to fight in World War I, women had taken their places in factories and businesses. During the four years of the war, women had become adept at earning a living outside the home. They did not want to leave their jobs when soldiers came back. And with the death of so many men during the war, some women were forced to continue supporting their families without the help of a man. The struggle to decide whether women would return to their old ways of life or to keep on with their newfound independence was another battle in the long campaign for women's rights. In the United States it led directly to women earning the right to vote in 1920.

Education

Throughout the 1920s education became a focus for youth and young adults alike. Increases in government and private funding allowed schools and colleges to offer more people a solid education than ever before. The increase in education also lead to more people participating in sports such as swimming, tennis, golf, and horseback riding that became part of college sports programs. With the middle class becoming wealthier, more young men and women could afford to go to college to train for better jobs. In the United States more than 150,000 college degrees were awarded to graduates by the end of the 1920s. The popularity of a college education during the decade focused attention on youth and new fashion styles emerged on college campuses throughout the United States and Europe.

Affordable luxury

Other changes altered everyday life in Europe and the United States. With a prospering economy and high employment, more people than ever had money to spend on entertainment. Automobiles were the most attractive luxury item, and anyone who could afford one had one. The Ford Motor Company had around ten thousand dealerships across the United States by 1924. People, especially Americans, hopped in their cars to explore their country, camping alongside the roads or staying in hotels at distant locations. Cars also offered people the opportunity to commute to work in the city from their homes in quiet suburbs or in housing developments surrounding urban areas. Radios gave people the opportunity to hear news about the world and became increasingly popular for entertainment. By 1925 music dominated 70 percent of the radio airwaves and reached more than 2.5 million American radio listeners. Other entertainment included films and music. People rushed to movie theaters to see the latest films; their popularity made movie actors and actresses into stars. A new type of music called jazz developed in

Rebellious young women of the 1920s often adopted several outrageous fashion fads.
© EVERETT COLLECTION INC./ ALAMY.

the United States, inspiring wild dance moves. And people could spend their money at newly constructed retail stores. By 1927 there were seventy thousand different retail locations throughout the United States, including A & P grocery stores, J.C. Penney department stores, Walgreen drugstores, and Fanny Farmer candy stores.

The beginning of Prohibition—an amendment to the U.S. Constitution in 1919 that made the manufacture, sale, or transportation of alcohol illegal—did not stop the energetic optimism of the decade, nor did it stop people from drinking. Although some Americans were happy to have a "dry" (alcohol-free) nation, many others supported the creation of speakeasies (illegal places selling alcohol and usually offering live music, dancing, and gambling, for late-night entertainment). So many speakeasies popped up around the country that the police could not effectively enforce Prohibition. By 1926 the sale of alcohol in the United States was estimated to be worth $3.6 billion, making many bootleggers, or people involved in the illegal manufacture and trade of alcohol, millionaires.

The relaxed feeling in the economy was fueled by governmental policies that let businesses grow and compete without much regulation. This, coupled with banking procedures that offered good terms to borrowers but little protection for investors, led to risky financial deals and the growth of many new companies. By the end of the decade the optimism that had inspired the creation of new businesses and investments could no longer sustain the economy and many businesses began to fail. With the stock market crash on October 24, 1929, a new era began: the Great Depression of the 1930s.

For More Information

Allen, Frederick Lewis. *Only Yesterday: An Informal History of the 1920s.* New York: Harper and Brothers, 1931. Reprint, New York: Wiley, 1997.

Hanson, Erica. *The 1920s.* San Diego, CA: Lucent Books, 1999.

Katz, William Loren. *The New Freedom to the New Deal, 1913–1939.* Austin, TX: Raintree Steck-Vaughn, 1993.

"The Roaring Twenties" *History.com.* http://www.history.com/topics/roaring-twenties (accessed on September 11, 2012).

Clothing, 1919–29

As the Western world celebrated the end of World War I (1914–18) clothing styles changed to reflect the enthusiasm of the time. The most striking differences came in the silhouettes, or shapes, of men's and women's outfits. In general, women's clothes went from flaring skirts to a tubular line, featuring flat chests and low waists, and men's clothes became much fuller, even baggy.

The changes in women's clothes came from new attitudes about life and work. During this decade women won the right to vote and many earned their own money. Women needed stylish clothes that they could wear to work or out during the day. For everyday wear women wore a tailored suit. For more festive occasions women wore clothes that were more comfortable and luxurious than before the war. The tight corsets that squeezed women into unnatural shapes were replaced with loose-fitting outfits and, eventually, by figure-skimming gowns with revealing necklines and open backs.

With the end of rationing clothes became elaborate. The most expensive were made of satin, silk, and brocade—a fabric with raised designs and adorned with ruffles, fringe, gathers, bows, jewels, and even fur. Women added fringed or transparent shawls to these outfits for even more decoration. Inspiration for women's clothing came from designers' ideas about the future. Designers created clothes that were very different from older styles. The most drastic change was the knee-length hemline. For the first time, women showed their legs in public, swinging them wildly to the new exuberant dances like the Charleston.

Narrower skirts to the knee and jackets with low waistlines gave women a new, tubular silhouette. © LEBRECHT/LEBRECHT MUSIC AND ARTS PHOTO LIBRARY/ALMAY.

Clothes also reflected the new art styles of the period. Bold geometric patterns and new designs were beaded, embroidered, and even painted on garments. The Orient and other cultures also inspired clothing styles, as seen with pajamas, the kimono sleeves of some dresses, and the turbans, or headwraps, complementing some outfits. The trend-setters for women were mostly fashion designers centered in Paris, France, including Gabrielle "Coco" Chanel (1883–1971), Madeline Vionnet (c. 1876–c. 1973), Paul Poiret (1879–1944), and Jean Patou (1880–1936). Although only the wealthiest women could wear original designer fashions, middle-class women would buy copies of French designs in retail stores, and other women bought patterns and yards of fabric to make their own.

For men, the decade offered similar style changes. Clothing became much looser. Men continued to wear the sack suit that became the most common style at the turn of the century, but the lines of the suit became smoother, with wider trousers belted high on the waist and broad-shouldered jackets. The widest men's pants were called Oxford Bags. The shirts men wore with their suits had attached collars by mid-decade and came in white and pastel shades of blue, tan, and yellow. Men's ties were no longer plain; they now featured stripes, polka dots, and plaids. Men no longer had to wear heavy fabrics in the heat of the summer. Gabardines (a twill fabric), flannels, and tweeds were replaced with light seersucker, a striped, lightly puckered linen or cotton. Seersucker was sewn into sack suits or made into a suit with a belted jacket to wear in hot weather. Men's fashions followed such trendsetters as Edward, Prince of Wales (1894–1972); pilot Charles Lindbergh (1902–1974); tennis players Jean René Lacoste (1904–1996) and Bill Tilden (1893–1953); swimmer Johnny Weissmuller (1904–1984); college football star Red Grange (1903–1991); movie star Rudolph Valentino (1895–1926); and countless college students on campuses throughout the United States and Europe.

In addition to the changes in the styles of everyday and formal wear, new styles emerged. Sportswear for men and women provided outfits for tennis, golf, swimming, boating, and other sports. Sports became so popular that styles for watching sports also became fashionable. Heavy raccoon coats were seen in the stands at college football games; derby hats topped men's heads at horse races and around town; and spectator shoes, a style of multicolored shoe, adorned the feet of people watching sporting events. The navy blue blazer also became associated with yachting clubs, among other things.

For More Information

Bigelow, Marybelle S. *Fashion in History: Apparel in the Western World.* Minneapolis, MN: Burgess Publishing, 1970.

Blum, Stella. *Everyday Fashions of the Twenties.* New York: Dover Publications, 1981.

Fass, Paula S. *The Damned and the Beautiful: American Youth in the 1920s.* New York: Oxford University Press, 1977.

Laubner, Ellie. *Fashions of the Roaring '20s.* Atglen, PA: Schiffer Publishing, 1996.

Influence of Youth on Fashion

The fast, wild, and showy decade of the 1920s is sometimes called the Age of Flaming Youth, because the influence and energy of young people was unleashed in a new way during this period. Young people met in high schools and colleges. They gathered and socialized in ways their parents and grandparents never could, and they created styles and fads that were imitated across the generations. In a world stunned by the devastation of World War I (1914–18), the fun and carefree freedom of the young was a welcome relief, and no style seemed too silly or frivolous to become high fashion.

World War I had raged throughout Europe, leaving almost an entire generation of young men dead or maimed. After the war, many young people rebelled against the values of their parents' generation, which they saw as having brought about the horrors of the war. They rejected the modesty, control, and respectability of the eras of the nineteenth and early twentieth centuries and embraced all that was modern, fast, and exciting. New inventions like the automobile (the Ford Model T began to be mass-produced in 1909) and new popular jazz music became symbols of the time. As the world recovered from death and destruction, many people celebrated being young and alive.

One thing that increased the influence of young people as a group was the growth of secondary education, or high school. The period following World War I was one of prosperity and industrialization. As more goods were mass-produced, people did not have to work as hard and childhood grew longer. By the 1920s many adolescents attended high school instead of working to help feed their families. For the first time, large numbers of young people spent a great deal of time together. College enrollment also increased during the 1920s. These high school and college students began to develop their own ways of dressing, talking,

Flatteners

Flatteners appeared on the fashion scene during the late 1910s and 1920s, around the same time as brassieres. However, while brassieres were designed to lift and support the breasts, flatteners had a different purpose: to press the breasts tightly against the body in order to give the wearer the flat-chested look that was popular at the time. Flatteners were made of cotton and elastic. Some laced up the sides to pull the breasts flat, while others had wide elastic bands at the breasts, stomach, and hips to hold the entire body in a fashionable slim shape. The latter type combined the features of the flattener with the corset.

During World War I (1914–18) women began working at higher paying jobs in order to replace the men who had gone to fight. These newly independent women were reluctant to return to their former and having fun. Films such as *The Campus Flirt* (1926) and *College Days* (1927) glamorized college life, and people everywhere began wearing raccoon coats and using college slang like the lighthearted students in the films. The college man and the flapper became the role models of the decade, and house parties, long drives, and dancing to jazz music became the most popular pastimes.

Another social change introduced by the youth of the 1920s was the idea of dating, or unchaperoned social engagements between men and women. In the years before the war, it was considered improper for men and women to spend time alone unless they were engaged. Even then, a chaperon, or older companion, was usually present when a man and a woman socialized. Dating introduced the idea that men and women could spend time getting to know each other in private even if they did not intend to marry. Dating might mean going to a party or nightclub for music and dancing or a drive in the car. It could also mean necking and petting,

nicknames for kissing and touching, that had been forbidden during the nineteenth century, but was viewed as good, clean fun by the young people of the 1920s.

Older, more conservative people were often shocked and scandalized by the behavior of the young during the Roaring Twenties. Besides dating and dancing in the modern close fashion, which many saw as immoral, youthful rebellion frequently included drinking illegal alcohol and using foul language. Young women began showing their knees, wearing heavy makeup, and smoking cigarettes. Many older community leaders tried to outlaw these disgraceful new practices, but, even more than alcohol and cigarettes, the freedom of the age was addictive, and the new liberated styles were unstoppable. When the stock market crash of 1929 introduced the more somber age of the Great Depression (1929–39), many conservative people claimed that the hard economic times were a punishment brought on by the excesses of the youth of the 1920s.

places in the home, or in poorly paid work. They began to demand more independence, and this included fighting for the right to vote and dressing in fashions that gave them more freedom of movement. While during the late 1800s and early 1900s, women had laced themselves into corsets that emphasized large breasts and hips, the ideal young woman of the Roaring Twenties was tall, thin, and boyish. The silhouette was called "tubular" because dresses were meant to be one straight tube hanging loose from shoulders to knees. Women who did not naturally have the popular boyish figure would strap themselves into restrictive undergarments. Because small breasts and hips were fashionable, many large-breasted women could only achieve the fashionable look by wearing flatteners that bound their breasts tightly against their bodies. In 1927 Sears sold a typical flattening corset called the Abdo-belt for $1.98. The corset reached from just above the breasts to just below the hips, had garters at the bottom for attaching stockings, and had wide elastic bands that slipped tightly over the bust and hips.

SEE ALSO *Volume 4, 1900–18: Brassiere*

For More Information

All the Rage. Alexandria, VA: Time-Life Books, 1992.

Bigelow, Marybelle S. *Fashion in History: Apparel in the Western World.* Minneapolis, MN: Burgess Publishing, 1970.

Blackman, Cally. *The 20s & 30s: Flappers & Vamps.* Milwaukee, WI: Gareth Stevens Incorporated, 2000.

Herald, Jacqueline. *Fashions of a Decade: The 1920s.* New York: Facts on File, 1991.

Formal Gowns

Ginger Rogers and Fred Astaire in a scene from the film The Gay Divorcee. The most glamorous evening gowns had flowing lines and elaborate ornamentation and swept the floor. © AP IMAGES

As the economies of Western countries began to recover after the end of World War I (1914–18), people began to be able to afford more luxurious clothes. The wealthiest women began to show off their riches through their clothes. Formal gowns, worn mostly for evening events, were their most elaborate outfits. Women's formal gowns during the first half of the 1920s were characterized by ornamentation. The most glamorous evening gowns were covered in jewels or intricate beadwork and swept the floor.

The taste for luxury spread from evening events to afternoon parties. As a result afternoon fashions made of expensive silk, brocade, satin, velvet, taffeta, and gold lamé, a shiny golden fabric, were soon as formal as evening wear. Dresses were embellished with lace, embroidery, ropes of pearls, and fur trimmings. Sashes, bows, ruffles, and drapes of sheer chiffon also added to the glamour of the gowns. As afternoon gowns became more formal, the hemline of the formal gowns could be anywhere from knee to floor length.

Gowns featured the long straight silhouette of an uncorseted thin figure, softened with occasional flounces, or strips of decorative cloth, gathers, or trailing panels made of long pieces of fabric that hung lower than the hem of the gown in back. By the mid-1920s gowns had developed flowing lines to show off and flatter the female figure. One feature of these gowns was a deep V-neck in the front and a deeper V in the back. Although the front was covered with an inset of contrasting fabric, the back showed off women's bare skin from shoulder to waist. By the late 1920s the gowns of the wealthiest women were spectacular, but women of more modest means also could wear beautiful, ready-made dresses from the retail stores that were scattered across the United States and Europe.

SEE ALSO *Volume 4, 1919–29: Hemlines*

For More Information

Drowne, Kathleen Morgan and Patrick Huber. *The 1920s*. Westport, CT: Greenwood Publishing, 2004.

Mulvagh, Jane. *Vogue History of 20th Century Fashion*. New York: Viking, 1988.

Hemlines

When World War I (1914–18) ended, women adopted a new style: the knee-length hemline. The year 1919 was the first year that European and American women showed their legs in public. Between 1919 and 1929 women's legs were seen beneath day, sport, and evening dresses.

The most fashionable silhouette, or shape, for a woman's skirt from 1919 to 1929 was straight and knee length. The skirts of the decade hid women's feminine curves with loose waists and sashes hugging the hips. These dresses created a silhouette that was worn best by the boyish figures of the young, especially the trendsetting flappers. The most fashionable shorter hemlines were worn most often by younger women, but some older, curvier women also adopted these fashions and began showing off their legs for the first time. More conservative, or reserved, women wore similar straight dresses with ankle-length hems.

Most dresses featured straight hemlines that neatly circled the upper calves. However, more flowing lines came into fashion later in the decade. The handkerchief hemline was created by circling the waist with an overskirt made of thin, transparent panels of fabric, which gave glimpses of the shorter straight hem of the tubular dress below. One corner of each fabric panel pointed toward the floor, giving the hemline an uneven look. Dresses and skirts with handkerchief hemlines hung below the knee.

Flappers

No decade in recent history has seen as much change in the status and style of women as the 1920s, sometimes called the Roaring Twenties or the Era of Wonderful Nonsense. Trendy young women of the 1920s were nicknamed flappers, and the flapper became the image that represented the tremendous change in women's lives and attitudes during that period.

During the early part of the twentieth century women in countries from Australia to Norway were gaining the right to vote, and more and more women were able to support themselves by working at jobs. In addition to women's new freedoms, by the 1920s there were automobiles to drive, films to see, and jazz music to dance to, and modern young women wanted to join in the fun. Young women were no longer content to spend hours binding themselves into burdensome layers of clothing or styling long masses of hair.

The term flapper originated in Great Britain, where there was a short fad among young women to wear rubber galoshes (an overshoe worn in the rain or snow) left open to flap when they walked. The name stuck, and throughout the United States and Europe flapper was the name given to liberated young women. Flappers were bold, confident, and sexy. They tried new fad diets in an effort to achieve a fashionable thinness, because new fashions required slim figures, flat chests, and slim hips. The flapper dress was boxy and hung straight from shoulder to knee, with no waist-line, allowing much more freedom of move-ment than women's fashions before the 1920s. While it did not show breasts or hips, it did show a lot of leg, and the just-below-the-knee length horrified many of the older genera-tion. French fashion designer Gabrielle "Coco" Chanel (1883–1971) did much to popularize the new freedom of the flapper look.

The mid-1920s saw the introduction of the short formal dress. Throughout most of the 1920s, the hemlines of evening dresses were the same knee-length lines as day dresses. Evening dresses of the period also featured handkerchief hemlines. By the end of the decade evening dresses began to show hemlines that hung slightly below the knees in front and trailed to the floor in back. Ankle-length evening gowns came into fashion in 1929 and have never really gone out of style since. But the preferred hemline length for day dresses has remained short for women of all ages since this time.

For More Information

Blackman, Cally. *The 20s & 30s: Flappers & Vamps*. Milwaukee, WI: Gareth Stevens Incorporated, 2000.

Ewing, Elizabeth. *History of 20th Century Fashion*. Lanham, MD: Barnes and Noble, 1974.

Flappers also shocked conservatives by cutting their hair short and wearing makeup. Before the 1920s long hair was the mark of a respectable lady, but flappers had no time for elaborate hairdos. They cut, or bobbed, their hair just below the ears and curled it in dozens of tiny spit curls with a new invention called a bobby pin. Some also used electric curling irons to create small waves called "marcels," named after Marcel Grateau (1852–1936), the French hair stylist who invented them. Cosmetics had long been associated with prostitutes and actresses, but flappers considered it glamorous to wear dark red lipstick, lots of rouge, and thick black lines around their eyes, sometimes made with the burned end of a matchstick. New cosmetics companies including Maybelline and Coty began manufacturing products to help women achieve the new look. For the first time, women began to carry cosmetics with them in handbags wherever they went.

One of the most famous flappers was silent film star Clara Bow (1905–1965). Sometimes called the "It" girl, Bow was thought to have "it," a quality of open sexuality, innocence, and fun that was the very definition of the flapper. Many women imitated Bow's look by drawing a bow shape on their lips, rimming their eyes in black, and curling their hair onto their cheeks.

Despite the youthful enthusiasm for the flapper style, some people felt threatened by it. When hemlines began to rise, several states made laws charging fines to women wearing skirts with hemlines more than 3 inches (8 centimeters) above the ankle, and many employers fired women who bobbed their hair. However, in the excitement and gaiety that followed the end of World War I in 1918, the movement toward a freer fashion could not be stopped by those who valued the old ways. It took the stock market crash of 1929 to bring the era of the flapper to a sudden end. Almost overnight, the arrival of an economic depression brought a serious tone to society. Women's hemlines dropped again, and the carefree age of the flapper was over.

Hoobler, Dorothy, and Thomas Hoobler. *Vanity Rules: A History of American Fashion and Beauty.* Brookfield, CT: Twenty-First Century Books, 2000.

Murray, Maggie Pexton. *Changing Styles in Fashion: Who, What, Why.* New York: Fairchild, 1989.

"Vintage Fashion–The History of Hemlines." *Glamour Daze.* http://glamourdaze.com/2010/12/vintage-fashion-history-of-hemlines.html (accessed on September 11, 2012).

Navy Blue Blazer

The first navy blue blazer, a type of jacket, appeared in the late 1830s. The designer of the blazer was the captain of the British ship the HMS *Blazer.* He had the jacket made out of navy blue serge, a smooth twill fabric, for his crew to wear for a visit from Queen Victoria (1819–1901). The double-breasted (two rows of buttons down the front) blazers sporting bright brass buttons impressed the queen immensely, and she made sure other sailors had blazers to wear.

Other men began to wear the navy blue blazer with brass buttons for sporting events that rose in popularity during the 1920s. The members of sport clubs, especially expensive yachting clubs, began wearing blue blazers with the emblem of their club sewn on the breast pocket. Colleges and preparatory schools in England and later in much of Europe and the United States adopted the navy blue blazer as part of their school uniforms by the end of the decade. While the blazers worn by the navy had flap pockets, school blazers had patch pockets, a separate piece of fabric sewn on top of the garment to form a pocket, and often featured the school crest embroidered in heavy gold thread on the breast pocket. Both types of jackets had brass buttons, which were embossed, or stamped, with the regimental, sporting club, or school emblem.

As the navy blue blazer became associated with those who could afford the membership fees of sporting clubs or the tuition of exclusive schools, more people began to wear them whether or not they were affiliated with a certain club or school. Blue blazers became common jackets for men's work attire by midcentury and an essential part of the preppy look that started in the 1950s and achieved its height in the 1980s.

SEE ALSO *Volume 5, 1946–60: Preppy Look*

For More Information
Keers, Paul. *A Gentleman's Wardrobe: Classic Clothes and the Modern Man.* New York: Harmony Books, 1987.
Schurnberger, Lynn. *Let There Be Clothes.* New York: Workman, 1991.

Oxford Bags
● ●

In the 1920s young people attempted to set themselves apart from their elders and establish their own fashion styles. In 1924 at Oxford University in Great Britain, a small group of male students began wearing trousers that never would have been worn by their fathers. These pants were loosely fitted and featured extremely wide legs; at their knees and cuffs they measured between 22 and 40 inches (56 and 102 centimeters) wide. They came to be known as Oxford Bags, named for their excessively baggy appearance and the institution of higher learning from which they originated.

Oxford Bags first were worn to get around the university's ban on wearing knickers, baggy trousers with legs gathered at the knees, in the classroom. Because of their size, Oxford Bags could be slid on effortlessly over the taboo knickers. The style allegedly was inspired by the type of pants that student oarsmen, or rowers, wore over their shorts.

Oxford Bags usually were worn with pullover turtleneck sweaters or short jackets. They were made of flannel and came in a range of colors. Some colors were more traditional: black, navy, beige, and gray; others, including pale green and lavender, were unique and attention-getting. A combination of their unusual style and color made Oxford Bags a fashion extreme of the decade, and they came to symbolize the recklessness of youth.

The Oxford Bag style soon grabbed the attention of American college students, particularly those attending the northeastern Ivy League schools, the American universities with the highest academic and social prestige. Undergraduates who were studying abroad and happened to be visiting Oxford began wearing them. Their popularity among more adventuresome American college students was solidified when, in January 1925, United States president Calvin Coolidge (1872–1933) declared that he "wouldn't be caught dead" wearing Oxford Bags. That spring, the John Wanamaker department store began marketing the trousers in the United States where they enjoyed some popularity among the young.

Because of the excessive nature of Oxford Bags, they never became a mainstream fashion trend and lost their appeal by the end of the 1920s. Pants that were excessively baggy, however, have come back in style at various points in time and have been trendy among the young. The trouser part of the zoot suit, which was popular among young, sporty African American males during the late 1930s and 1940s, the bell-bottoms that were favored by young men and women during the late 1960s, and the wide-legged jeans worn by male adolescents in the 1990s and into the twenty-first century all featured extremely baggy pants.

SEE ALSO *Volume 4, 1930–45: Zoot Suit; Volume 5, 1961–79: Bell-Bottoms*

The young man on the left is wearing loose-fitting, wide-legged Oxford Bags, often considered extravagant. © UK HISTORY/ALAMY.

For More Information

Keers, Paul. *A Gentleman's Wardrobe: Classic Clothes and the Modern Man.* New York: Harmony Books, 1987.

McEvoy, Anne. *The 20's and 30's.* New York: Chelsea House, 2009.

Pajamas

Pajamas were loungewear and sleepwear that consisted of pants and jacket tops. The word derived from two Hindi terms: "pa(y)," for leg, and "jamah," for garment. It entered the English language around 1880 as "pyjamas," after the British colonized India, where Hindi was spoken. Americans adopted the term from the British as "pajamas."

Pajamas for men, women, and children became popular in the United States during the 1920s. For men, they replaced nightshirts, which were one-piece long-sleeved shirts that flowed down to or below the knees. Men's pajamas were loose fitting. The trousers had drawstrings around the waist, or were fastened by a few buttons in the front. The tops were collarless or with a relaxed collar that could remain undone or be buttoned closed. Tops had a line of buttons down the front or were held closed by overlapping the front panels across the chest and tying a sash around the waist. Men's pajamas were made of cotton, silk, or rayon, which then was called artificial silk. Men who wanted warmth against winter nights chose heavyweight cotton flannel pajamas. Although conservative dressers wore solid, drab-colored sleep outfits, many others chose pajamas in stripes and lively prints. The Smithsonian Institution in Washington, D.C., holds a rather colorful pair of pajamas worn by American president Warren G. Harding (1865–1923) in the early 1920s. They are turquoise silk with white leaves that are appliquéd, or attached, onto the garment.

Women envied the comfort of men's pajamas and, in the liberated atmosphere that followed World War I (1914–18), adopted the attire to their own lifestyles. Women wore pajamas for sleeping and also for lounging about the home and the beach. Most women's pajamas were made of flowing fabrics such as silk, satin, chiffon, or rayon. They featured loose, ankle-length pants that hung straight at the bottom or were drawn tight around the ankle by a ribbon or lacing. The waistlines of the pants had drawstrings. Tops were hip-length jackets with varying sleeve lengths. A home sewing pattern sold by the Butterick

Pajamas could be made out of expensive fabrics such as silk and were popular attire for lounging at the beach. © JOHN SPRINGER COLLECTION/ HISTORICAL/CORBIS.

Publishing Company of Massachusetts offered the seamstress a choice of necklines: rounded, squared, or with a rounded collar. Women's pajamas sometimes were quite stylized, even whimsical. For instance, on occasion they were designed in silk in an Oriental fashion that featured loose, wide sleeves like kimonos, the loose robes worn by Japanese men and women. They were printed colorfully with renderings of Japanese and Chinese objects, such as paper lanterns, geisha (female entertainer) houses, and chopsticks. Children wore pajamas primarily for sleeping. The styles were similar to adult garments.

Pajamas have not always been restricted to the home and beach. In the early 2010s, the trend of wearing pajamas around town became very popular among American youth. Elizabeth Holmes pointed out in the *Wall Street Journal* that sales of pajamas, sweatshirts, and sweatpants among thirteen- to seventeen-year-olds were up dramatically over previous years, with many retailers prominently displaying loungewear looks in their storefronts. This trend was further fueled by Hollywood celebrities wearing pajama outfits even to formal evening events, turning heads and creating news headlines in the process. In 2011 Farhad Manjoo, writing for online magazine *Slate,* noted that screenwriter, actress, and director Sofia Coppola was photographed wearing her Louis Vuitton designer pajamas out during the day, and in the same year, designer Rachel Roy wore a pair of traditional-looking striped pajamas to a movie premiere, as reported by Caitlin Petreycik of *InStyle!* In fact, so popular was the trend that one official in Louisiana's Caddo Parish, noted by Holmes, called for an ordinance that would prohibit wearing pajamas in public altogether. Manjoo pointed out that even back in 1929, an incident involving pajamas being worn in public caught the public's attention when a barber from New Jersey, Samuel Nelson, made a wager that he could walk in his pajamas from Newark to Irvington without getting arrested. Although he lost his bet, he ultimately prevailed in court when the judge threw out the case, advising the arresting officer that "Neither you nor I are censors of modern fashion here."

SEE ALSO *Volume 2, Early Asian Cultures: Kimono*

For More Information

Cunnington, C. Willett, and Phillis Cunnington. *Handbook of English Costume in the Seventeenth Century.* Boston, MA: Plays, Inc., 1972.

Holmes, Elizabeth. "Why Not Wear Pajamas All Day?" *Wall Street Journal,* January 19, 2012. http://online.wsj.com/article/SB100014240529702045 55904577168762962727568.html?mod=WSJ_hp_mostpop_read (accessed on September 3, 2012).

Manjoo, Farhad. "The Pajama Manifesto." *Slate,* January 25, 2012. http://www.slate.com/articles/life/a_fine_whine/2012/01/pajamas_in_public_the_popularity_of_sleepwear_is_not_a_sign_of_america_s_declining_moral_fiber_.html (accessed on September 3, 2012).

Payne, Blanche, Geitel Winakor, and Jane Farrell-Beck. *The History of Costume.* 2nd ed. New York: HarperCollins, 1992.

Petreycik, Caitlin. "Rachel Roy Wore Pajamas to a Premiere: Here's Why." *InStyle!* August 9, 2011. http://news.instyle.com/2011/08/09/rachel-roy-pajamas-one-day/ (accessed on September 3, 2012).

Plus Fours

First introduced during the 1920s, plus fours were a variation on the traditional knee pants called knickerbockers, (or knickers), which had been worn by men, boys, and, occasionally, women, since the late 1800s. Plus fours received their name because they were made 4 inches (10 centimeters) longer than ordinary knickers. While they still fastened with a tight band at the knee, the extra fabric of the plus four bloused over the band, giving a relaxed, baggy look. Plus fours were an extravagant, careless style that fit right in with the looser fashions and lifestyles of the 1920s. They also offered more freedom of movement than previous knickers, which made them extremely popular with sportsmen, especially golfers.

During World War I (1914–18) certain British officers wore loose riding breeches, or pants, which bloused out over the tops of their boots. The dashing look their baggy pants gave them caused the fashion to spread when the war ended. Edward VIII (1894–1972), then the Prince of Wales, brought the fashion to the United States on a visit in 1924. Within a very short time plus fours had replaced regular shorter knickers, which were soon considered old-fashioned. Plus twos, which used less fabric than plus fours, and plus sixes, which used more, also were introduced but did not become as popular as the plus fours.

The sport of golf had been played for centuries, but the 1920s saw the creation of golf fashion. Golfers not only wished to play well but to appear dashing and stylish. They quickly adopted the new plus fours, which were not only in style but also had extra length that gave athletes more room to move than previous knickers. The fashionable golfer of the 1920s wore plus fours with argyle knee socks and a pullover sweater. (Argyle is a traditional knitted pattern with large interlocking diamonds in various colors that gave a flashy look to the sportsman.)

The popularity of plus fours declined in the mid-1930s, when walking shorts were introduced. However, they have never quite disappeared from the fashion scene, particularly among golfers. The early 1980s saw a revival of plus fours on such famous golfers as American Payne Stewart (1957–1999), who wore them throughout his career.

A golfer wearing plus fours, pants baggier and 4 inches longer than ordinary knickers.
© AP IMAGES.

SEE ALSO *Volume 4, 1900–18: Knickers*

For More Information

Laver, James. *Costume and Fashion: A Concise History.* New York: Thames and Hudson, 2002.

Yarwood, Doreen. *Fashion in the Western World: 1500–1900.* New York: Drama Book Publishers, 1992.

Raccoon Coat

For a short time during the mid-1920s, wearing long, bulky coats of raccoon fur was a fad among young American men and some young women, especially those attending colleges and universities. Distinctive and flamboyant, the gray and black raccoon fur coat fit perfectly with the style of the Roaring Twenties, a period following World War I (1914–18) in which people experienced newfound freedoms and a sense of rebellion, and dressed in flashy and extravagant fashions.

Animal fur, with its warm insulation, had long been a popular winter coat material, and raccoon was one of the least expensive types of fur. Raccoon coats became especially popular in the 1920s when driving became one of the most popular activities for those wealthy enough to own Henry Ford's Model T automobile. Full-length raccoon fur coats were perfect for winter driving because cars were mostly open in the 1920s and driving could be very cold in the winter. The privileged few who could afford a car also wore raccoon coats, and subsequently made raccoon coats a symbol of wealth.

It wasn't long before college students joined in the raccoon coat fad. Eventually the coats would be closely identified with students, especially students at the Ivy League colleges and universities, which were Brown, Columbia, Cornell, Dartmouth, Harvard, University of Pennsylvania, Princeton, and Yale. Popularized by such celebrities as radio star Rudy Vallee (1901–1986), football hero Red Grange (1903–1991), and the famous college football players from Notre Dame nicknamed the "Four Horsemen," young people began wearing raccoon coats to football games and college parties. Modern young men who listened to jazz music, used modern slang, and wore raccoon coats with straw hats called boaters and white spats (a cloth or leather covering) on their shoes, were nicknamed "collegiates" or "sheiks."

Raccoon coats were not only popular among wealthy young university men. Women, enjoying a new fashion freedom in the 1920s, also liked to wear the warm, dashing coats, and for young African Americans

By wearing a raccoon coat, college football star Red Grange, right, helped to launch a campus craze. © UNDERWOOD & UNDERWOOD/HISTORICAL/ CORBIS.

raccoon coats were the height of style. James Van Der Zee (1887–1983), a well-known African American artist, caught much of the spirit of the decade in a painting of a fashionable young black man and woman standing by their car, titled *Couple in Raccoon Coats.*

Raccoon coats are considered, along with flappers, the Charleston dance, and the Model T Ford, to be a symbol of the short-lived fads of the 1920s. The coats were heavy and bulky, and by the end of the decade they had been replaced by lighter weight camel's hair coats. The raccoon coat did have a brief revival during the late 1950s, when fashionable women once again sought vintage, or antique, 1920s coats. An article in the Fall 1956 issue of *Gentry* magazine pointed out that unlike other fashion revivals where certain elements were modified or modernized, the raccoon coat had resisted such modifications and returned to popularity in its original format.

For More Information

Pendergast, Sara and Tom Pendergast. *Bowling, Beatniks, and Bell-bottoms:1920s and 1930s.* Detroit, MI, Gale, 2002.

Schoeffler, O. E., and William Gale. *Esquire's Encyclopedia of 20th Century Men's Fashions.* New York: McGraw-Hill, 1973.

"Undergraduate Prestige." *Gentry* (Fall 1956): 100.

Spectator Sports Style

Attending sporting events was a popular leisure time practice during the 1920s. Fashion-conscious spectators dressed in attire appropriate for a variety of sporting events. Often fashion was dictated by the weather. For instance, male and female college students who attended autumn and early winter football games wore bulky raccoon fur coats or heavy tan-colored camel hair and woolen polo coats belted at the waist or with a partial belt at the back. By the late 1920s women's sportswear was becoming more masculine, and as a result, college-aged women wore tailored woolen tweed suits with knee-length skirts and loose-fitting slacks to collegiate sporting events.

Warm weather events such as horse races often were held in stylish surroundings such as resorts. Wealthy male spectators wore navy blue woolen blazers with gold buttons. In the late 1920s men and women began wearing black-and-white "spectator shoes." They were white wing-tipped leather shoes trimmed with black leather or patent leather at the toes and heels. Women wore spectator pumps with matching spectator handbags, white leather rectangular pocketbooks with a clasp at the top and black leather or patent leather trim at the four corners.

In 1927 Charles Lindbergh (1902–1974) became the first aviator to fly solo across the Atlantic Ocean. He became an instant popular cultural hero to millions of Americans. By 1928 fans of Lindbergh bought mass-produced reproductions of his leather aviator jacket to wear during sporting events.

Golf matches also were fashionable places to see and be seen. Men watching the golf games wore clothes that mimicked the players' outfits: three-piece sports suits that featured knickers (loose-fitting pants that ended just below the knees, usually fitted at the bottom by a button), a vest, and a jacket. These often were made of light-woven woolens or tweeds. Knickers were worn with colorful argyle (diamond-shaped pattern) knee socks. Many of the accessories to golf attire, such as ties, caps, and socks, often were fashioned from Scottish clan tartans, as the game of golf was developed in Scotland.

For tennis matches spectators wore variations of tennis players' garb. The major difference was that tennis players wore white only. Men often wore soft, loose-fitting white woolen flannel trousers with a navy blazer. Women wore knee-length pleated summer dresses in white or pastels, or loose trousers with pleats in the front. During the late 1920s many women chose to wear berets, or soft, wide rounded woolen caps with narrow headbands, with their spectator-style clothing.

For More Information

Peacock, John. *Men's Fashion: The Complete Sourcebook.* London, England: Thames and Hudson, 1996.

Peacock, John. *20th Century Fashion.* London, England: Thames and Hudson, 1993.

Sportswear

During the 1920s many men and women began to participate in such sports as golf, tennis, and swimming. Affluent people also enjoyed yachting and polo. To provide comfort and ease of movement, new styles of sportswear were designed. Additionally, with young people increasingly aware of style trends, sportswear designs reflected the spirited, celebrity-conscious sensibilities of the decade.

Charles Lindbergh

Young and handsome, modest and daring, Charles Lindbergh was one of the first mass-media celebrities. After performing the amazing feat of flying solo from New York to Paris, France, in his small airplane in 1927, Lindbergh became an international hero, adored by millions and hounded by the press. Lindbergh gained fame not only for his flight, but because he represented qualities of adventurous boldness that were highly valued during the 1920s. It was a time of new achievements and modern inventions, and, by flying across the Atlantic Ocean, Lindbergh had opened up a new world of possibilities.

Lindbergh was born in Detroit, Michigan, in 1902. His father, a lawyer, and his mother, a science teacher, raised him in the small farm community of Little Falls, Minnesota, where young Charles learned independence very early. He began driving an automobile at the age of eleven and later dropped out of the University of Wisconsin to learn to fly airplanes. He loved flying and soon had a job flying mail from St. Louis, Missouri, to Chicago, Illinois. In 1927, when a New York hotel owner offered twenty-five thousand dollars to the first pilot to fly alone across the Atlantic, Lindbergh was determined at once to try. On May 21, 1927, he took five sandwiches and a bottle of water in his plane, the *Spirit of St. Louis,* and took off from New York's Roosevelt Field.

Lindbergh had sought to win money and fame for his accomplishment, but he had no idea what awaited him. When he landed, thirty-three hours later, in Le Bourget Field in Paris, more than 150,000 people had gathered to greet him. From that moment on he was a public figure, and newly created forms of mass media gave Lindbergh a kind of fame that no public figure had seen before. When Lindbergh returned to the United States, President Calvin Coolidge (1872–1933) presented him with medals. Millionaire Harry Guggenheim (1890–1971) paid for Lindbergh to fly his plane on a three-month tour of the United States, where he visited forty-eight states and gave more than one hundred speeches in ninety-two cities. He was the hero of dozens of parades. Crowds followed him wherever he went. Admirers copied his clothes; his flight started a fad of wearing leather jackets and loose aviator pants. A popular new fast dance was called the "Lindy hop," because it made the dancers feel like they were flying. Several U.S. toymakers made "Lucky Lindy" dolls that looked like Lindbergh. When he married Anne Morrow (1906–2001) in 1929, reporters in motorboats followed them on their honeymoon cruise. A shy person, Lindbergh

Famous athletes inspired some of the more popular styles of sportswear. American tennis star Bill Tilden (1893–1953) wore white lightweight woolen flannel slacks and cable-stitched white or cream-colored sweaters. From 1920 to 1926, the years in which he won seven consecutive Davis Cup matches, Tilden set the style for men's tennis attire. In 1927 French tennis star Jean René Lacoste (1904–1996), nicknamed the Crocodile for his perseverance, beat Tilden to win the Davis Cup for France. Not only did he become the new champion, but he became the reigning tried to avoid media attention when he could. He refused many offers that could have led to more fame, such as an offer from American newspaper publisher William Randolph Hearst (1863–1951) for five hundred thousand dollars to star in movies.

Lindbergh and his wife continued to fly and to speak in favor of aviation all over the world. People were enchanted by the beautiful young couple and followed their adventures closely. However, the Lindberghs' celebrity had tragic results. In March 1932 their twenty-month-old son, Charles III, was kidnapped, and his dead body was found ten days later. Lindbergh always blamed the constant focus of the press for drawing the kidnapper's attention to his family. The kidnapping and the trial that followed it in 1934 were huge media events, followed closely by people all over the world.

Trying to escape his own fame, Lindbergh spent several years in Europe. He visited Germany frequently, and Hermann Göring (1893–1946), a high Nazi official, presented him with a German medal of honor. When he came back he spoke out against the United States' involvement in World War II (1939–45). Many people thought his speeches were pro-Nazi and anti-Jewish, and Lindbergh's popularity fell dramatically. He did join in the war effort, in the Pacific, where he went as a civilian, or nonmilitary, adviser and managed to fly fifty combat missions.

Charles Lindbergh's leather aviator jacket and pants inspired a fashion trend. © THE LIBRARY OF CONGRESS.

Lindbergh spent most of the rest of his life quietly with his family, though he continued to fly and to promote air travel. A lifelong inventor, he also helped a doctor friend invent a special pump for use in organ transplants. Lindbergh died of cancer on the island of Maui in Hawaii in 1974.

fashion trendsetter as well. Like Tilden and other tennis and polo players, Lacoste wore a cotton polo shirt, a short-sleeved, pullover, knit shirt with a turned-over collar, for maximum upper torso movement. Beginning in the mid-1920s, Lacoste decorated the left side of the chest with a crocodile embroidered logo, reflecting his nickname. This was the first instance of a trademark appearing on the outer side of a garment, and the fad caught on with Lacoste's fans. Tennis players who cheered for Lacoste were inspired to wear polo shirts with crocodiles just like his own. Lacoste eventually partnered with a knitwear manufacturer to market polo shirts decorated with embroidered crocodile logos for tennis, golf, and sailing.

Style-conscious golfers wore knickers, loose-fitting pants that ended just below the knees. They often were worn with colorful argyle (diamond-shaped patterned) woolen knee socks. By 1925 men wore three-piece sports suits, consisting of jacket, vest, and knickers or plus fours, for golf games and for casual wear at resorts.

Thanks to the freer moral code of the decade, swimsuits for men and women became more lightweight and followed the line of the torso. They allowed for more athleticism in swimming, rather than simply bathing in a bulky garment while at the beach or in a pool.

Women's sportswear followed general trends toward the boyish look. For tennis, women wore pleated, knee-length white skirts with sleeveless white tops. For golf they wore pleated skirts of various solid colors and plaids with knit tops and short or long-sleeved cardigans, sweaters that button up the front. French designer Gabrielle "Coco" Chanel (1883–1971) introduced loose bell-bottomed trousers, pants that flare at the bottoms of the legs, for women to wear while sailing or yachting. These pants looked like trousers worn by sailors. This style was controversial since women did not wear trousers, even for physically demanding sports in which the range of movement required made skirts cumbersome.

SEE ALSO *Volume 4, 1919–29: Plus Fours; Volume 4, 1930–45: Polo Shirt*

For More Information

Drowne, Kathleen Morgan and Patrick Huber. *The 1920s.* Westport, CT: Greenwood Publishing, 2004.

Gaines, Ann. *Coco Chanel.* Philadelphia, PA: Chelsea House, 2003.

Peacock, John. *Men's Fashion: The Complete Sourcebook.* London, England: Thames and Hudson, 1996.

Peacock, John. *20th Century Fashion.* London, England: Thames and Hudson, 1993.

Wallis, Jeremy. *Creative Lives: Coco Chanel.* Chicago, IL: Heinemann Library, 2002.

Swimwear

Swimwear is clothing worn while swimming or visiting the beach or a pool. As more and more men and women visited public beaches to swim, relax, and play recreational water sports in the late nineteenth and

Women display different bathing costumes from the early twentieth century. © ROSSEFORP/IMAGEBROKER/ALAMY.

early twentieth centuries, issues about swimwear arose regarding popular fashion, functionality, and modesty.

The early years of the twentieth century were daring ones for women's swimwear design. Bulky suits with pant and skirt combinations were replaced by loose, one-piece suits that fit snugly against the body. They featured short skirts that covered the frontal area like aprons. In 1907 Australian swimmer Annette Kellermann (1887–1975) was arrested on a beach in Boston, Massachusetts, for indecent exposure. She was wearing a black, formfitting, sleeveless, apronless woolen suit with a scooped neckline and opaque black stockings. By 1910 the Kellermann suit was embraced by young women, although more conservative females chose one-piece suits with an attached modesty skirt. Men's suits were bulky two-piece cotton or woolen garments with vests that covered most of the chest, torso, and legs down to the shins or ankles. Many featured skirt-like coverings.

By 1916 swimwear was a popular form of fashion. That year the first annual "Bathing Suit Day" was held at Madison Square Garden in New York City, where new styles of swimwear were modeled. For the first time, men's and women's swimwear was viewed as sporty, trendy, and even sexually appealing. At that time aprons began to disappear on fashionable suits. Still, regulations on many public beaches required men and women to wear lightweight untucked tops and skirts or skirt-like covers over the fitted shorts.

Jantzen Knitting Mills of Portland, Oregon, began manufacturing men's and women's suits made of a rubberized rib-stitched fabric that held its formfitting shape wet or dry and did not retain water. They were inspired to create this new style of suit by a male rower searching for a functional suit. This suit also was appealing to the many young people of the post–World War I (1914–18) period who sought to make sports and recreation a bigger part of social life. The company patented this swimsuit in 1921. The suits were manufactured on special automated circular knitting machines similar to those used to make hosiery. The Jantzen advertising slogan, "the suit that changed bathing into swimming," reflected its recreational appeal.

In the 1920s the short apron skirt disappeared, as did stockings for females. Men's and women's swimsuits actually resembled each other. Both covered the torso and were sleeveless and formfitting. Early in the decade, women wore one- or two-piece knit suits with vest-shaped tops, scooped necks, and shoulder straps, called maillot style. Later, a more conservative one-piece California suit with a sleeveless top and skirt was fashionable. Along with the changes in fit, swimwear began to feature bold designs and colors. Instead of the dark black or blue suits of the past, swimwear began to be made in bright colors. Art deco, a type of modern art, also began influencing swimwear styles, and novelty suits with sleek art deco animal adornments became popular.

SEE ALSO *Volume 3, Nineteenth Century: Bathing Costumes; Volume 5, 1946–60: Bikini*

For More Information

Bigelow, Marybelle S. *Fashion in History: Apparel in the Western World.* Minneapolis, MN: Burgess Publishing, 1970.

Drowne, Kathleen Morgan and Patrick Huber. *The 1920s.* Westport, CT: Greenwood Publishing, 2004.

Probert, Christina. *Swimwear in Vogue Since 1910.* New York: Abbeville Press, 1981.

Tailored Suit for Women

At the turn of the twentieth century tailored suits for women, consisting of a matching or co-ordinated jacket and skirt, were popular outfits for office work, afternoon social visits, travel, and leisure activities such as walking. For the first few decades of the 1900s, tailored suits were made up of loose-fitting waist-length or hip-length jackets and ankle-length or floor-length flared skirts. Jackets often were adorned with buttons, fabric belts, and sailor collars, collars resembling those worn by sailors in the United States Navy, with narrow front folds and a large rectangle at the back of the neck. They were worn with shirtwaists, or tailored blouses. The suits of this era often were made of many yards of heavy material. The skirts were so long and full that they picked up dirt from floors and outdoor paths.

After World War I (1914–18), as women moved more freely in society, tailored suits remained fashionable. However, in order to allow for more movement, the tailored suit of the 1920s was tapered in its cut. The new, less bulky look weighed less and was less burdensome for movement.

By the early 1920s the French-inspired boyish look was fashionable. This style, which de-emphasized the curves of the female form, was popular among young American women who

A woman wearing a tailored suit. © SASHA/HULTON ARCHIVE/GETTY IMAGES.

lived liberated lifestyles and were called flappers. Jackets still frequently featured buttons and sailor collars, but the cut was plain and straight or tubular, with no emphasis on a woman's bust or waistline. Jacket waistlines were dropped from the natural waist, with the belt of the suit loosely hugging the hips. Skirts had lost their flare but were slightly gathered at the back. Instead of hemlines that hugged the ankle or the ground, skirts ended at mid calf. By 1925 skirts hung perfectly straight and hemlines ended at the knee or just below the knee. These outfits often were worn with tailored blouses and cloches, bell-shaped, deep-crowned hats.

French fashion designer Gabrielle "Coco" Chanel (1883–1971) had the greatest influence on the styling of the tailored suit for women in the 1920s. Her suits featured short, straight skirts or skirts with soft pleats. The Chanel jacket ended at the hip and had a square or boxy look. The neckline was collarless, and the fabric around the neckline and front of the jacket was trimmed discreetly with narrow braiding or ribbon. The jacket occasionally had buttons or fasteners but was worn open. Tailored blouses often were worn untucked with a fabric or leather belt at the hipline.

For More Information

Chaney, Lisa. *Coco Chanel: An Intimate Life*. London, England: Penguin Group, 2011.

Gaines, Ann. *Coco Chanel*. Philadelphia, PA: Chelsea House, 2003.

Peacock, John. *20th Century Fashion*. London, England: Thames and Hudson, 1993.

Wallis, Jeremy. *Creative Lives: Coco Chanel*. Chicago, IL: Heinemann Library, 2002.

Waugh, Norah. *The Cut of Women's Clothes*. New York: Theatre Arts Books, 1994.

Headwear, 1919–29

After the end of World War I (1914–18) both men and women were inspired to change their hairstyles. For men the changes were not too drastic, but for women hairstyles were dramatically different. Nevertheless, both men and women prized neatly groomed hairstyles during this period.

Soldiers came back from the war with military cuts, hairstyles trimmed close on top and shaved up past the ears in the back. Men grew their hair out a bit but maintained neat, short hair. It was not the cut but the dressing that distinguished men's hair in the 1920s. Men smeared grease on their hair to create a shiny patent leather look popularized by movie stars. Only older men wore beards, while young men shaved daily, leaving only a pencil-thin mustache, if any facial hair at all.

Women, having experienced independence from men during the war, marked their continued desire for this freedom with a new hairstyle. Snipping off the long tresses that men so admired, women signaled their desire for liberation from their old roles in society. The bob, or short haircut, became the most popular style of all classes of women. Usually only old women and men did not like bobbed hair. In *Fashions in Hair: The First Five Thousand Years* Richard Corson quotes an article in a 1926 *Good Housekeeping* magazine that remarked about "How pleasant they are to look at—the proud, smoothly-coiffed, youthful, brave, bobbed topknots of today, hair brushed and clipped until it outlines charmingly the back of the head! So different they are from the grotesque shapes and sizes we have seen since the twentieth century ushered in the towering pompadour. Here is simplicity and a lightness of head…. Hats are easy to buy, headaches from hairpins and heavy coils disappear, and hairdressing takes less time—though more thought." Bobs were styled in several different ways, teased to look windswept, slicked close to the head, or sculpted into flat waves. As quoted by Corson, actress Mary Pickford (1893–1979) summed up a good reason women cut their hair, writing, "Of one thing I am sure: [a woman] looks smarter with a bob, and smartness rather than beauty seems to be the goal of every woman these days." In 1926 the most daring and controversial of hairdos, the Eton crop, came into fashion. This was a severe, masculine style with hair slicked back close to the head. Many older, more conservative women and the majority of men disliked the Eton crop as a move against traditional femininity. Haircutting had become such a phenomenon by the end of the decade that in the United States alone the number of barbershops had increased from eleven thousand to forty thousand.

Both men and women wore hats between 1919 and 1929. For women the cloche hat and bandeau were stylish additions to a bobbed head. For men the fedora and derby hats topped men's neat styles.

For More Information

Amphlett, Hilda. *Hats: A History of Fashion in Headwear.* New York: Dover, 2003.

Corson, Richard. *Fashions in Hair: The First Five Thousand Years.* London, England: Peter Owen, 2001.

Trasko, Mary. *Daring Do's: A History of Extraordinary Hair.* New York: Flammarion, 1994.

Bandeau

Women's short hairstyles during the 1920s were not without ornament. Small metal clasps with sparkling real or fake jewels held hair off the face or elaborate headdresses completely covered the hair. One especially popular adornment was the bandeau, a band circling the head at the brow to hold the hair. The word *bandeau* is the French diminutive term for "band" or "strip." The bandeau could be a simple, plain cloth or a jeweled band. A plain bandeau was often worn for playing sports or with casual outfits. With especially fancy outfits, women wore bandeaus made of glittering fabric and sometimes stuck a feather or fastened a large jewel to the bandeau in the middle of the forehead. Bandeaus varied in width from about .5 inch to 4 inches (1 to 10 centimeters). In modern usage, bandeau often refers to a type of undergarment or bathing suit top that encircles the breasts, rather than the popular hairband of the 1920s.

For More Information

Batterberry, Michael, and Ariane Batterberry. *Fashion: The Mirror of History.* New York: Greenwich House, 1977.

Bigelow, Marybelle S. *Fashion in History: Apparel in the Western World.* Minneapolis, MN: Burgess Publishing, 1970.

Contini, Mila. *Fashion: From Ancient Egypt to the Present Day.* Edited by James Laver. New York: Odyssey Press, 1965.

McEvoy, Anne. *The 1920s and 1930s.* New York: Chelsea House, 2009.

Clean-Shaven Men

For many centuries men allowed their facial hair to grow. In the early decades of United States history, such public figures as politicians and businessmen often sported beards or mustaches. In an act of rebellion during the 1890s, British artist-illustrator Aubrey Beardsley (1872–1898), Irish poet William Butler Yeats (1865–1939), and Irish poet-playwright Oscar Wilde (1854–1900) shaved their faces. It was not until after World War I (1914–18) that shaving became fashionable. By then a modern, well-groomed male was a clean-shaven male.

Men grew their facial hair for several, logical reasons: it was annoying and difficult to remove on a regular basis and doing so could be, quite literally a bloody affair. Men who attempted to be clean-shaven employed a straight razor. While this method had been around for centuries, it was perfected in the nineteenth century with the invention of alloys such as "silver steel" by British scientist and inventor, Michael Faraday. He found that by adding 0.02 percent silver to 99.98 percent steel, he could create a blade that was both shinier and more flexible than steel alone. A straight razor generally consists of a folding stainless steel blade and a handle that was traditionally made from bone, ivory, celluloid, and in later years, plastic. Using the razor would require careful sharpening using a strop, which was a long strip of leather that would hone the razor's edge much finer than a sharpening stone ever could. A man would then lather up his face using special shaving soap. Then, holding the skin taut, the blade would be held at a thirty-degree angle,

The clean-shaven man only became popular in the 1920s. Before then, being clean shaven was considered an act of rebellion. © THE LIBRARY OF CONGRESS.

shaving in a downward motion. If the blade was held too flat, the hair would be ripped out rather than cut; if it was held too steep, the skin would be nicked. The exacting precision required for a good, clean shave made it rather cumbersome to all but the most dedicated.

The shaving process became easier and safer during the nineteenth century with the invention of the T-shaped safety razor, in which the skin was exposed only to the edge of the blade; the safety razor also angled the blade at a fixed, optimal position to minimize cuts and nicks. The trend toward shaving, however, may be most directly linked to King Camp Gillette (1855–1932). In 1895 Gillette, a traveling salesman, originated the concept of a disposable razor blade. Working with engineer William E. Nickerson (1853–1930), he created a thin, replaceable double-edged blade, which was patented in 1901 and immediately marketed. Previous blades were sharpened when they became dull. Gillette's blades were disposable and were safe and inexpensive.

At the time most men were shaved by barbers; they occasionally shaved themselves at home, peering into small mirrors before lathering up their faces. They favored some form of facial hair if only because they could not be bothered to shave themselves, or be shaved, every day. During World War I Gillette struck a deal with the U.S. armed forces, which issued a safety razor and disposable blades to each soldier. While on combat duty, shaving one's face was practical, and potentially lifesaving, because it allowed the soldier to more safely close and seal his gas mask. Thus, hundreds of thousands of young men simultaneously became adept at shaving themselves. At the war's end each soldier was allowed to keep his razor and Gillette began mass-producing replacement blades for this ready-made market of men who shaved daily. Although straight-razor shaving was still common and quite popular until the 1950s, in the latter half of the twentieth century people favored disposable safety razors, a trend that still continues. In the twenty-first century, small pockets of straight-razor shaving aficionados still exist and continue the traditional art, but it is mainly seen as a hobby and leisure pursuit.

Adding to the popularity of the clean-shaven look was the development of the electric shaver in the 1920s and its subsequent marketing during the following decade. With the advent of the electric shaver, men found it even easier to remove their facial hair without having to depend upon water, soap, and razor blades.

SEE ALSO *Volume 4, 1930–45: Electric Shaver*

For More Information

Adams, Russell B. *King C. Gillette, the Man and His Wonderful Shaving Device.* Boston, MA: Little, Brown, 1978.

Barlow, Ronald S. *The Vanishing American Barber Shop.* El Cajon, CA: Windmill Publishing Company, 1993.

Dowling, Tim. *King Camp Gillette: Inventor of the Disposable Culture.* London, England: Short Books, 2001.

"Straight Razor History—A Brief Guide through the Years." *The Invisible Edge.* http://www.theinvisibleedge.co.uk/page81.html (accessed on September 3, 2012).

"Straight Razor Shaving Tips." *The English Shaving Company.* http://www.theenglishshavingcompany.com/english-shaving-tips.html (accessed on September 3, 2012).

Cloche Hat

● ●

Cloche hats were the most fashionable form of women's headwear during the 1920s. They were close-fitting, helmet-shaped hats that had deep rounded crowns with no brim or just a small curve at the edge. *Cloche* means "bell" in French, and these hats were so named because they resembled large bells. They often were made of woolen felt.

Women's hats of the early twentieth century were ornately decorated with deep crowns and wide brims. During World War I (1914–18) hats became less flamboyant. By the end of the war many women were cutting their long hair. They wore bobbed haircuts trimmed to the nape of the neck; shingled locks, layering their short hair into flat, overlapping rows; and the Eton crop, a severe, masculine style with hair slicked back close to the head.

With new short hair fashions, older style hats appeared old-fashioned and out of place. The tight helmet fit of the cloche hat

A woman wearing a cloche hat, which fit snugly against the fashionable short haircuts of the time. © CSU ARCHIVES/ EVERETT COLLECTION INC./ ALAMY.

complemented the new hairstyles. The round crown of the cloche followed the natural curve of the head. Trims were simple. Some cloches were trimmed with a ribbon band and some featured small jeweled brooches on one side or in front. Others were unadorned. Women wore their cloche hats pulled down over to just above their eyes so that the forehead was hidden under the hat. The back of the cloche hat skimmed the nape of the neck. Sometimes the cloche was worn tilted over the right eye. The cloche hat gave women an air of mysterious appeal, but wearing the hat so low made watching where one walked difficult. To counteract that problem, women began holding their heads back as they walked, a mannerism that led to a new slant in female posture. Cloche hats became very popular attire for weddings. Such bridal accessories were trimmed in lace or composed solely of veiling.

During the 1930s cloche hats still were popular but in modified versions. Some had pleated folds on the sides and back, and some dipped over one eye. Trims of veiling or lace sometimes were added, as hat fashions returned to more elaborate designs. The cloche faded from fashion in the late 1930s and 1940s but has since seen sporadic revival as a fashion trend.

For More Information

Bates, Karen Grigsby. "Luke Song's Hats Grab Attention—Even Aretha Franklin's." *Los Angeles Times*, April 12, 2009. http://www.latimes.com/ features/image/la-igw-hatsong12-2009apr12,0,7941463.story (accessed on September 3, 2012).

Bowles, Hamish. "Haute Couture Fall 2009: Hamish Bowles's Favorite Chanel Look." *Vogue,* July 8, 2009. http://www.vogue.com/vogue-daily/article/vd-haute-couture-fall-2009-hamish-bowless-favorite-chanel-look/ (accessed on September 3, 2012).

Langley, Susan. *Vintage Hats and Bonnets, 1770–1970.* Paducah, KY: Collector Books, 1998.

Moore, Booth. "1920s Era Roars Back in Fashion and in Film." *Denver Post,* December 22, 2011. http://www.denverpost.com/lifestyles/ci_19595998 (accessed on September 3, 2012).

Probert, Christina. *Hats in Vogue Since 1910.* New York: Abbeville Press, 1981.

Derby

Derby hats were rigid head coverings that traditionally were made of woolen felt. They featured slender, rolled brims and rounded, or dome-shaped, tops. Conventional, or traditional, derbies primarily were worn by men. The traditional colors were black, gray, and brown. Derbies usually featured a matching silk ribbon band tied at the side with a flattened bow.

Derby hats were named for Edward Stanley (1752–1834), the twelfth earl of Derby. In 1780 the earl organized a horse race. The race was held on a track in Epsom, near London, England. It became an annual event, whose participants were three-year-old horses, and it became known as the Epsom Derby. The term derby came to refer to any important race for three-year-old horses. In the United States similar races, most famously, the Kentucky Derby, were named for the Epsom Derby. The style of hat known as the derby was worn by many stylish Englishmen who attended the Epsom Derby. Americans identified the hats with the races and thus the nickname stuck.

Comedian Charlie Chaplin in character as the Tramp, wearing a derby.
© INTERFOTO/ALAMY.

The hat Americans named derby was in fact a bowler hat, a style introduced in England during the 1850s. Bowlers became popular in Great Britain and crossed the Atlantic to the United States during the mid-nineteenth century where they became known as derbies. Primarily they were stylish hats for refined, upper-class, well-dressed gentlemen. In the late nineteenth century derbies began to be worn by men and women for horseback riding and hunting.

Beginning in the 1910s derbies were worn by dapper, or elegant, American men for office and evening wear. By the 1920s they shared popularity with wider-brimmed fedora hats as attire for the successful banker or businessman. They entered American popular culture in the 1929 gangster novel *Little Caesar,* by W. R. Burnett (1899–1982), where a character is described as "the man in the derby hat." At the time derbies were adopted by a number of jazz musicians, actors, gangsters, and even traveling salesmen. Also, two of the famed Brown Derby Restaurants, where movie stars of the 1920s and 1930s gathered, were built in Hollywood and Beverly Hills, California, in 1926 and 1931. The buildings were constructed in the shape of huge derby hats, immortalizing the fashion trend. In the early 1930s derbies found an even broader market, becoming the hats of choice for men of all classes who wanted to wear a hat more stylish than common fedoras or woolen caps. The popularity of derbies declined in the late 1930s.

SEE ALSO *Volume 3, Nineteenth Century: Bowler*

For More Information

Bigelow, Marybelle S. *Fashion in History: Apparel in the Western World.* Minneapolis, MN: Burgess Publishing, 1970.

Robinson, Fred Miller. *The Man in the Bowler Hat: His History and Iconography.* Chapel Hill, NC: University of North Carolina Press, 1993.

Fedora
●●●

During the nineteenth century and the first half of the twentieth century, hats and caps were a necessary part of a well-dressed man's daily wardrobe. Between the 1890s and the 1960s, one of the most popular hats was the fedora, a soft felt hat with a brim and tapered crown with a crease down the center. For several decades fashionable bachelors, conservative family men, politicians, and even gangsters all wore fedora hats whenever they left home.

The fedora is a descendent of a traditional brimmed hat that was part of the customary costume of the Tyrol, a mountainous region in Austria. The first modern fedora appeared in France, onstage in an 1882 play by Victorien Sardou (1831–1908). The play was called *Fedora,* which also was the name of the heroine, played by the extremely popular actress Sarah Bernhardt (1844–1923). As Fedora, Bernhardt wore a stylish soft felt hat with a crease in the crown. Bernhardt's many fans were charmed and began to wear the new hat, called a fedora in honor of the star's role. While fedoras were first popularly worn by women in France, Germany, and England, they were soon adopted by men as an alternative to the stiff bowler hats, or derby hats, that were the most common men's hats at the time.

By the 1920s fedoras were everywhere. Though the fedora had at first been a casual hat, during the 1920s Britain's Prince of Wales, later King Edward VIII (1894–1972) changed the fashion by wearing a fedora with dressy suits. The hat he wore when he visited the United States in 1924 was copied and mass-produced by Sears Roebuck. Soon most well-dressed American men wore a fedora.

Orchestra leader Count Basie sporting a fedora with the brim turned down. Although popular in the 1920s fedoras made a comeback as an accessory during the 2010s. © AP IMAGES.

One of the most popular features of the hat was its softness and ability to be shaped by the individual wearer. From the shape of the crown to the "snap" of the brim, each wearer could shape the hat to show his own personality. Gangsters, members of a criminal gang, and dapper young men might wear the brim turned down so it covered the wearer's eyes, while a more practical working man might turn the brim up to keep rain from running down his collar. Even the crease in the crown could be shaped to an individual's preference. Fedoras were usually brown, black, or gray, though some flamboyant dressers wore them in white, blue, and even lilac.

Although men's styles are usually slow to change, there were some differences in the look of the fedora through the years, mostly in the shape of the crease and the width of the brim. Wider brimmed hats were popular from the 1920s through the mid-1940s and narrower brims from the late 1940s up to the 1960s. By the 1960s hats for men had largely gone out of style as everyday wear, and fedoras began to be seen as relics of a more fashionable past.

Even so, the fedora saw a revival in pop culture in the 1980s when the main characters in the *Indiana Jones* and *Nightmare on Elm Street* film franchises wore fedoras. In addition, pop singer Michael Jackson made the style part of his iconic look for his *Bad* album. Although the popularity of fedoras once again waned in the 1990s, they appeared on fashion runways in the late 2000s, inspiring such celebrities as Kate Moss, Cameron Diaz, Justin Timberlake, and Keira Knightley to sport the accessory. Besides traditional solid colors, fedoras in the 2010s can be found in plaid and pinstriped patterns and are often made of straw or canvas instead of felt.

For More Information

Schoeffler, O. E., and William Gale. *Esquire's Encyclopedia of 20th Century Men's Fashions*. New York: McGraw-Hill, 1973.

Patent Leather Look
● ●

Men had for some time carefully groomed their hair to give it shine. But in the 1920s a smooth glossy finish called the patent leather look became very popular. Film stars such as Rudolph Valentino (1895–1926) and George Raft (1895–1980) wore the patent leather look and helped spread its appeal. Men slicked down their short hair with grease to make the flat, perfectly styled look. Some men added a stiff wave to their plastered-down hair. Most men parted their hair on the side, but some men, especially those losing their hair, used a center part. The patent leather look was worn most often with a clean-shaven face but a pencil-thin mustache could also accompany the look. The look was a perfect example of the desire for men to wear short, neatly-styled hair throughout the decade.

For More Information

Corson, Richard. *Fashions in Hair: The First Five Thousand Years*. London, England: Peter Owen, 2001.

Drowne, Kathleen Morgan and Patrick Huber. *The 1920s*. Westport, CT: Greenwood Publishing, 2004.

Shingle

The shingle was considered the most feminine women's short hairdo of the 1920s. The style featured short hair worn close to the head with the front and the sides cut to cover the ears and the back cut and shaped into layers of short fringe at the neckline to resemble shingles on a roof. The sides were cut at a slant, with the shortest hair at the nape of the neck and the longest hair falling at the bottom tip of the earlobe and forming a curl. The hairdo was parted at the center or on the side. The shingle hairdo sometimes was waved a bit, and it was less flat and heavy looking than the bluntly cut bob, an extremely short haircut.

The shingle was created in 1914 by Polish-born, Paris-based hairdresser Monsieur Antoine, also known as Antoine de Paris (born Antek Cierplikowski; 1884–1977), who was hairstylist to several of Europe's most renowned actresses. Monsieur Antoine designed the shingle hairstyle especially for Irene Castle (1893–1969), a trendsetting American ballroom dancing star who was performing in Paris, France. The style quickly caught on in Europe, and by 1927 Monsieur Antoine opened an elegant hair salon in New York City and formally introduced the shingle cut, or shingle bob, to wealthy American women. At the same time the shingle cut also was introduced to millions of movie fans when it was worn by film star Louise Brooks (1906–1985). After admiring the onscreen hairdo of Brooks, thousands of young women asked their hairdressers to give them shingle cuts. The shingle hairstyle remained stylish into the early 1930s, and then its popularity gave way to looser, more traditionally feminine mid-length hairdos.

For More Information

Drowne, Kathleen Morgan and Patrick Huber. *The 1920s*. Westport, CT: Greenwood Publishing, 2004.

Turudich, Daniela. *Art Deco Hair: Hairstyles of the 1920s and 1930s*. Long Beach, CA: Streamline Press, 2003.

The shingle was a popular hairstyle of the 1920s. The sides were cut at a slant, with the hair longest at the tip of the earlobe. © GENERAL PHOTOGRAPHIC AGENCY/ HULTON ARCHIVE/GETTY IMAGES.

Short Hair for Women

In an April 1927 issue of *Pictorial Review,* a well-known opera singer of the 1920s named Mary Garden (1874–1967) wrote an article titled "Why I Bobbed My Hair," explaining to her fans why she cut off her long hair. She said, "Bobbed hair is a state of mind and not merely a new manner of dressing my head…. I consider getting rid of our long hair one of the many little shackles that women have cast aside in their passage to freedom." This statement expresses the underlying reason behind the 1920s fad of short hair for women. While until World War I (1914–18) long and carefully styled hair had been a symbol of elegant femininity, never cut except in times of serious illness, during the Roaring Twenties, a time of rebellion and newfound freedoms following the calamities of World War I, short hair on women became a symbol of liberation, fun, and daring.

There is a legend that the imaginative French fashion designer Gabrielle "Coco" Chanel (1883–1971) started the short hair fad one night when she was about to go out to the opera. The gas heater in Chanel's apartment exploded, burning off most of her long hair. The spirited designer supposedly trimmed off the burnt ends into a sassy short hairdo, then continued with her evening out, starting a fashion that swept much of the Western world. Though this story is probably fictional, it captures the spirit of the short-haired flappers of the 1920s, creative and bold young women, determined to get on with their lives.

However it began, the short hair trend spread quickly as women discovered the pleasure of a haircut that was easy to maintain. During the 1920s the number of haircutting salons rose from five thousand to twenty-three thousand, with some women even going to men's barbershops for their haircuts. Hair became shorter and shorter, ranging from the bob, which was chin-length, to the boyish Eton crop. Some women curled their hair in small spitcurls, using bobby pins, a newly invented hairpin that was

Short hair on women was a symbol of liberation, fun, and daring. © H. ARMSTRONG ROBERTS/CLASSICSTOCK/ ALAMY.

named after bobbed hair. Hot irons were used to make Marcel waves, named after Marcel Grateau (1852–1936), the French hair stylist who invented them. Soon only the old or the very conservative had long hair.

However, those who did not like to see the changes either in fashion or in the status of women fought against the new styles. Conservative clergymen preached against bobbed hair, while some doctors claimed that cutting their hair would cause women to go bald. Many shop owners fired saleswomen who cut their hair.

After the U.S. stock market crash in 1929, the general mood of society became much more somber. The excitement and confidence of the 1920s ended, and women returned to a softer look, which included longer hair.

For More Information

Blackman, Cally. *The 20s & 30s: Flappers & Vamps*. Milwaukee, WI: Gareth Stevens Incorporated, 2000.

Garden, Mary. "Why I Bobbed My Hair." *Pictorial Review* (April 1927): 8.

Hoobler, Dorothy, and Thomas Hoobler. *Vanity Rules: A History of American Fashion and Beauty*. Brookfield, CT: Twenty-First Century Books, 2000.

"Trends in Bobbed Hair including the 1920's." *1920–30.com.* http://www.1920-30.com/fashion/the-bob.html (accessed on September 11, 2012).

Body Decorations, 1919–29

After World War I (1914–18) both women and men changed the way they adorned themselves. No longer needing to follow the rules set by the military, men began getting their fashion guidance from newly popular film actors and public figures, such as the Prince of Wales, later King Edward VIII (1894–1972), or created their own styles on college campuses throughout Europe and the United States. The decade brought more changes for women than for men.

Women began to experiment with makeup. Bold use of cosmetics marked the decade as women created dramatic looks that imitated movie stars such as Clara Bow (1905–1965) and Theda Bara (1885–1955). Women traced their eyes with black eyeliner, plucked their eyebrows out and drew new ones with a dark pencil, and reshaped the line of their lips with red pencil to make them look like a cupid's bow. To complement their heavily painted faces, women slicked bright polish on their fingernails and adorned themselves with many accessories.

The accessories of the decade were influenced by many different sources. Women wore jewelry inspired by the unearthing in 1922 of the ancient Egyptian pharaoh Tutankhamen, who lived in the fourteenth century B.C.E., and by the new art movements sweeping Europe and the United States, including cubism, art deco, and surrealism. The creation of costume jewelry allowed women to wear bigger, bolder jewels and to follow trends without spending a fortune. Brand names also became important during the decade, especially with the introduction of Chanel No. 5 in 1921, which would become the world's most famous perfume.

For More Information

Dorner, Jane. *Fashion in the Twenties and Thirties*. London, England: Ian Allan Ltd., 1973.

Grafton, Carol Belanger. *Shoes, Hats, and Fashion Accessories: A Pictorial Archive, 1850–1940*. Mineola, NY: Dover Publications, 1998.

Laver, James. *Costume and Fashion: A Concise History*. 4th ed. London, England: Thames and Hudson, 2002.

Payne, Blanche, Geitel Winakor, and Jane Farrell-Beck. *The History of Costume*. 2nd ed. New York: HarperCollins, 1992.

Chanel No. 5, introduced in 1921, remains one of the world's most popular fragrances. © TOBI JENKINS/ ASSOCIATED NEWSPAPERS/REX FEATURES DAILY MAIL/REX/ ALAMY.

Chanel No. 5

Chanel No. 5 has become one of the world's most popular fragrances. Chanel No. 5 was the first synthetic, or man-made, perfume. Instead of essential oils from nature, synthetic perfumes are made with an aldehyde, an organic compound that yields alcohol when reduced. Synthetic perfumes offer unique smells and more stable bases that make the products more concentrated and longer lasting.

The history of perfume dates back to the ancient civilizations. By the start of the twentieth century, natural essence perfumes were being sold in elaborately designed bottles at affordable prices by such French companies as Coty, D'Orsay, Guerlain, Lanvin, Lubin, Molinard, and Roger and Gallet. In early 1921 French fashion designer Gabrielle "Coco" Chanel (1883–1971) commissioned Russian perfume chemist Ernest Beaux, the former perfumer to the Russian royal family, to create several new fragrances. The best would be packaged and sold by La Maison Chanel, or the House of Chanel. Beaux presented Chanel with five new synthetic fragrances. Chanel tested each one and chose the fifth bottle. That is how Chanel No. 5 received its name.

Gabrielle Chanel, being the superstitious type, released the first simple, square-lined bottles of Chanel No. 5 for sale on the fifth day of the fifth month of 1921. The perfume was an immediate success, and by 1924 Chanel had an entire perfume division with Ernest Beaux as its technical director. Beaux went on to create other iconic Chanel perfumes, such as Chanel No. 22 in 1922, Cuir de Russie in 1924, Gardenia in 1925, Bois des Îles in 1926, Soir de Paris in 1928, and Kobako in 1936.

The popularity of Chanel No. 5 continued throughout the rest of the century. The perfume became immortalized in the public's mind as being associated with Hollywood's most famous actress, Marilyn Monroe. In 1952, in a *LIFE Magazine* article, Marilyn related her response to a question she had been asked by an interviewer: "Once, this fellow says, 'Marilyn, what do you wear to bed?' So I said I only wear Chanel No. 5 and he groans, 'Oh no, I can't use that.'" That little anecdote served as a huge boost to the perfume's sales. Since the 1960s, Chanel has used a number of high-profile stars to endorse Chanel No. 5. In 1968 print ads featured model and actress, Lauren Hutton. In 1969 it was Cheryl Tiegs. Other stars that have promoted Chanel are Catherine Deneuve (1976), Carole Bouquet (1987), Vanessa Paradis (1991), Estella Warren (2001), Nicole Kidman (2004), and Audrey Tautou (2008).

By the twenty-first century a bottle of Chanel No. 5 sold every thirty seconds. The company continues to use celebrities to endorse its signature product, appearing in ad campaigns around the world. In 2012 Brad Pitt became the first male celebrity to endorse Chanel No. 5, according to *E! Entertainment.*

For More Information

"Audrey Tautou New Face of Chanel." *China Daily*, May 16, 2008. http://www.chinadaily.com.cn/lifestyle/2008-05/16/content_6690516.htm (accessed on September 3, 2012).

"Coco Nuts: The Women of Chanel No. 5." *Elle,* April 24, 2009. http://www.elle.com/beauty/coco-nuts-the-women-of-chanel-no-5-319422 (accessed on September 3, 2012).

Coolidge, Carrie. "Chanel No. 5 Wins the Readers' Choice Award for Best Fragrance." *Luxist,* June 1, 2010. http://www.luxist.com/2010/06/01/chanel-no-5-wins-the-readers-choice-award-for-best-fragrance/ (accessed on September 3, 2012).

"Hollywood Topic A-Plus Whole Town's Talking about Marilyn Monroe." *LIFE Magazine,* April 7, 1952. http://books.google.com/books?id=ElYEAAAAMBAJ&pg=PA101&source=gbs_toc_r&cad=2#v=onepage&q&f=false (accessed on September 3, 2012).

Madsen, Axel. *Chanel: A Woman of Her Own.* New York: Henry Holt, 1990.

Gabrielle "Coco" Chanel

Probably the most important fashion designer of the twentieth century, Gabrielle "Coco" Chanel (1883–1971) created the basic look of the modern woman. That look, like one of Chanel's classic suits, has remained original and vibrant from the 1920s, when it first appeared on French fashion runways, into the twenty-first century. Chanel's success as a timeless designer comes from her very practical approach to women's fashions. Real elegance, according to Chanel, came from feeling comfortable and free in one's clothes. The point of fashion, she insisted, was to allow the real woman to show through, not to cover her up with frills and fluff.

Gabrielle Chanel was born into poverty to unmarried parents in the small French town of Saumur. Her father was never a part of her life, and her mother died when Gabrielle was twelve, leaving her to spend the rest of her youth in an orphanage. The nuns there taught the young girl only one skill: sewing. Gabrielle was energetic, spirited, and determined to leave the orphanage and her deprived childhood behind her. As a young woman she earned the nickname "Coco" from the word cocotte, a French word for a woman with loose morals.

Chanel used her sewing skills and a fine eye for design to create hats that were simple and stylish, unlike the elaborate, plumed (ornamental) hats French women were wearing. Soon she opened a hat shop in Paris, France, and began to design clothes as well. In 1909 she created the House of Chanel, her own fashion design company. Chanel's designs came from watching people relax at the seaside and in the country. Deciding that women needed comfort and freedom of movement just as much as men did, she eliminated the confining corset, a restrictive undergarment, and helped define the concept of "sports clothes," clothes that could be worn at a variety of informal occasions. She used fabrics formerly considered low-class and too practical to be fashionable, like jersey knits and wools to create beautiful, expensive dresses and suits.

Some of Chanel's most enduring contributions to women's fashions were the simple knit suit and the "little black dress," a simple black cocktail dress that is still often

Newman, Cathy. *Perfume: The Art and Science of Scent.* Washington, DC: National Geographic Society, 1998.

Serpe, Gina, and Ken Baker. "Brad Pitt Is Modeling for Chanel No. 5!" *E! Online,* May 8, 2012. http://www.eonline.com/news/314627/brad-pitt-is-modeling-for-chanel-no-5 (accessed on September 3, 2012).

Costume Jewelry

Adornments for the body that are not made from precious materials or stones are called costume jewelry. Costume jewelry provides an inexpensive way to add glamour and sparkle to fashion because it is usually considered a basic of any woman's wardrobe. In 1926 she shocked some and thrilled others by adding trousers for women to her clothing line. During the mid-1920s she also joined with famed perfumer Ernest Beaux to create the scent that would become her signature, Chanel No. 5.

The worldwide economic depression of the 1930s dealt a blow to the House of Chanel, and during the occupation of France by the Germans during World War II (1939–45), Chanel closed her design business. She reopened in 1954, reintroducing many of her classic designs, such as a navy blue suit in wool jersey. However, her European customers did not appreciate Chanel's return to simplicity after the war, when other designers were using frills and other ornaments to emphasize femininity. But American women continued to love the practical and stylish new fashions. Chanel suits and copies of Chanel suits were very popular with American women, including influential First Lady Jacqueline Kennedy Onassis (1929–1994), during the early 1960s, causing many Europeans to rethink their criticisms.

Chanel continued to work and design until her death at age eighty-eight. The House of

Gabrielle "Coco" Chanel created the basic look of the modern woman. © CSU ARCHIVES/EVERETT COLLECTION INC./ALAMY.

Chanel continues to operate in the twenty-first century, carrying on its founder's tradition of breezy elegance and practical style.

made of cheap materials, such as glass or plastic rather than diamonds and emeralds, and plain steel, brass, or copper, rather than gold and silver. Though costume jewelry has been worn for centuries, it had a major rise in popularity during the 1920s and 1930s.

For as long as people have worn jewelry made of precious stones and metals, they have also made fake versions of that jewelry. Even ancient Greeks and Romans wore glass jewelry, which imitated the look of expensive precious stones. During the seventeenth and eighteenth centuries French and English jewelers worked to perfect new hard types of glass that could be cut to give the many-faceted look of a diamond. This glass was called paste, and paste became the name given to false jewels.

Jewelry made of paste was sometimes called "fashioned" jewelry, because the stones were made, or fashioned, by people rather than being naturally occurring substances that could be mined or excavated.

During the early 1920s the creative French designer Gabrielle "Coco" Chanel (1883–1971) introduced many popular new styles. She moved away from the formal layers of clothing that had been popular during the 1800s, considering them old-fashioned and suffocating. Chanel's styles were simple, loose, and comfortable, and to dress them up with sparkle she designed a type of fashioned jewelry she named costume jewelry.

Chanel's costume jewelry was big and bold with long strings of glass beads, dangling earrings, and many plastic bracelets stacked up on the arms. The inexpensive flashy jewels fit right in with the sexy look of the 1920s flapper, or independent and rebellious woman, and soon costume jewelry adorned many stylish young women across the Western world. Other well-known designers, such as Elsa Schiaparelli (1896–1973) of Italy, began to design their own styles of costume jewelry.

The tremendous popularity of costume jewelry lasted through the 1930s, as many women imitated the glamour of Hollywood stars. Though women continue to buy costume jewelry as an inexpensive alternative to real jewelry into the twenty-first century, many of the costume pieces designed during the costume jewelry craze of the 1920s have become collectors' items, commanding prices far higher than what they originally sold for.

For modern-day collectors of vintage costume jewelry, aside from Chanel there are a number of notable brands that attract a fair amount of interest. These include Boucher, Carnegie, Coro, Eisenberg, De Rosa, Du Jay, Haskell, KJL, Mazer, Swarovski, and Trifari. Trifari deserves special mention, as its vintage pieces are as unique as they are captivating. They have been worn by many famous people over the years, such as First Lady Mamie Eisenhower, who specially commissioned jewelry from Trifari for two inaugural balls, and singer/actress Madonna, who wore 1920s-inspired Trifari pieces in the film *Evita*.

SEE ALSO *Volume 3, Eighteenth Century: Paste Jewelry*

For More Information

Brower, Brock. "Chez Chanel: Couturiere and Courtesan, Coco Made Her Own Rules as She Freed Women from Old Fussy, Frilly Fashions." *Smithsonian* (July 2001): 60–66.

"Costume Jewelry Designers & Company Information." *Antiquing Online—The Jewelry Box.* http://www.antiquingonline.com/jewelry-designers.htm (accessed on September 3, 2012).

Haedrich, Marcel. *Coco Chanel: Her Life, Her Secrets.* New York: Little, Brown, 1972.

"The History of Trifari Jewellery." *Maenad's Gems.* http://jewellerysales.maenads-gems.co.uk/html/trifari_history.html (accessed on September 3, 2012).

"Michelle Obama & G-20's Other First Ladies: Who Was Best-Dressed?" *Huffington Post,* June 27, 2010. http://www.huffingtonpost.com/2010/06/27/michelle-obama-g-20s-othe_n_627028.html#s106802&title=President_Obama_and (accessed on September 3, 2012).

Miller, Brandon Marie. *Dressed for the Occasion: What Americans Wore 1620–1970.* Minneapolis, MN: Lerner Publications, 1999.

Miller, Judith. "Learn More About…Trifari Jewelry." *DK Books.* http://www.dk.co.uk/static/cs/uk/11/features/miller/learnmore02.html (accessed on September 3, 2012).

N&N Vintage Jewelry. http://www.trifari.com/ (accessed on September 3, 2012).

Schiffer, Nancy, and Lyngerda Kelley. *Costume Jewelry: The Great Pretenders.* Atglen, PA: Schiffer Publishing, 1998.

Wallach, Janet. *Chanel: Her Style and Her Life.* New York: Doubleday, 1998.

Wallis, Jeremy. *Coco Chanel.* Chicago, IL: Heinemann, 2001.

Yarwood, Doreen. *Fashion in the Western World: 1500–1900.* New York: Drama Book Publishers, 1992.

Makeup

Substances applied to the face for the purpose of enhancing, improving, or highlighting the features of the face are called cosmetics or makeup. People have used cosmetics since very ancient times, and the use of cosmetics, like other fashions, is usually driven by the social customs and beliefs of the day. Though during certain periods men have worn makeup, in modern times it has usually been considered a decoration for women only. The liberated fashions of the 1920s introduced an era of acceptance of makeup as a part of women's costume that has continued into the twenty-first century.

One effect of cosmetics is that they highlight the sexuality of the women who wear them, by emphasizing lips and eyes and reddening cheeks. Therefore, for much of the nineteenth century those of the middle and upper classes did not consider makeup respectable. By the early decades of the twentieth century the view of cosmetics began to change. Women gained the right to vote in many places and began to

Using makeup to emphasize lips, eyes, and cheeks reflected a new sense of women's freedom. © SILVER SCREEN COLLECTION/ MOVIEPIX/GETTY IMAGES.

gain other freedoms as well. The start of World War I in 1914 had brought a more public role for many women, as they took over the jobs left empty by men who had gone to war. When the war ended in 1918, these modern, more independent women were not content with the old styles. They wanted fashion that was fun, sexy, and free, and the generous use of cosmetics was part of the new, daring image. Modern young women of the 1920s, called flappers, used heavy lipstick in dark reds with names like oxblood. They reddened their cheeks with rouge, and since hemlines were going up, many rouged their knees as well.

In addition to women's new freedoms, Western European and American fashion also was influenced by an interest in Eastern styles, which were viewed as foreign and exotic. Just before World War I, much of Western society was fascinated with the Russian ballet, which featured bright costumes with Oriental designs and heavy, dark makeup. While fashion designers copied the Russian costumes, stylish women copied their makeup, and some even had their lips, cheeks, and eyebrows permanently tattooed with dark colors. In 1922 archeologists (scientists who study the distant past using physical evidence) discovered the treasure-filled tomb of the ancient Egyptian pharaoh Tutankhamen, who ruled in the fourteenth century B.C.E. The excitement over the discovery brought an Egyptian look into fashion, which included heavy eyeliner circling the eyes.

Women such as Elizabeth Arden (1884–1966), Madame C. J. Walker (1867–1919), and Helena Rubenstein (1870–1965) formed companies to sell the newly popular cosmetics. Cosmetics began to be packaged in portable containers, such as tubes for lipstick and decorative flat containers called compacts for powder. It not only became fashionable for women to carry cosmetics with them wherever they went, but, for the first time, stylish women applied their makeup in public, using a small mirror in the lid of their powder compact.

SEE ALSO *Volume 4, 1900–18: Lipstick*

For More Information

Bigelow, Marybelle S. *Fashion in History: Apparel in the Western World.* Minneapolis, MN: Burgess Publishing, 1970.

Hoobler, Dorothy, and Thomas Hoobler. *Vanity Rules: A History of American Fashion and Beauty.* Brookfield, CT: Twenty-First Century Books, 2000.

Hunt, Jilly. *Popular Culture: 1900–1919.* Chicago, IL: Raintree, 2013.

Nail Polish

The fashion of decorating the fingernails and toenails with color began in ancient societies, mainly among those of the upper classes. Carefully tended and adorned nails showed that one belonged to a leisure class that did not have to do manual labor. By the early twentieth century, advances in industry had made many products more affordable to a wide range of people, and luxuries, such as cosmetics and nail polish, became available to those of all classes. This, along with advances in paint technology that allowed the creation of a hard durable paint, caused an increase in the popularity of colored polish for fingernails and toenails by the 1920s.

Around 3000 B.C.E. wealthy people in ancient China used a mixture of beeswax, egg whites, gelatin, and dyes to paint their fingernails red, black, gold, and silver. Ancient Babylonians and Egyptians also colored their nails with natural substances such as henna powder, a reddish powder or paste made from the dried leaves of the henna bush, using color to indicate the wearer's rank in society. Even men in Egypt and ancient Rome sometimes painted their nails and lips red before going into battle.

During the late nineteenth century in Europe and the United States, it became common for people to manicure their nails, using scissors and files to trim and shape them. Colored creams and powders were rubbed into the nails for decoration, but they wore off quickly. It was not until the introduction of the automobile, and the shiny, durable paints that were created to protect its metal surfaces, that modern fingernail polish was introduced. Made much the same as automobile paint, the first liquid nail polish appeared in 1907 and was soon available in a variety of bright colors. The flashy style of the 1920s, with its love of exotic Eastern fashions, was the perfect time for the new product, and young women of the era painted their nails in bright pinks and reds, sometimes leaving the tips white for contrast.

One of the first brands of nail polish sold in the United States was Cutex Liquid Polish. Women's magazines, such as the *Ladies' Home Journal* and *Delineator,* carried advertisements to entice women to use Cutex. One Cutex ad in the *Delineator* of September 1929 features the celebrity dancer Irene Castle (1893–1969) showing off painted nails. The ad copy reads: "The celebrated Irene Castle McLaughlin finds this new polish flatters her lovely hands. Tomorrow's fashion is what Irene Castle McLaughlin is doing today! That was true even when she was a mere girl. The world caught its breath when she bobbed her hair … and scissors clicked from coast to coast. She improvised new steps and the whole world danced them." The fashion for painted nails has not diminished. Cutex and many other brands of nail polish continue to be sold throughout the world.

In the twenty-first century, social attitudes regarding gender roles have been slowly changing, and this is reflected in changing perceptions of the appropriateness of makeup for men, including nail polish. The American clothing company, J.Crew, sparked controversy with its 2011 product catalog, which contained a photo of the company president, Jenna Lyons, with her young son, whose toenails were painted neon pink. British R&B musician, Seal, actress Jessica Alba's husband Cash Warren, actor and singer Zac Efron, guitarist Dave Navarro, and actor Johnny Depp are all male celebrities who have been seen and photographed wearing nail polish in public.

This has, in turn, brought attention to a number of companies that sell cosmetics to both genders. In 2011 a new American company, Alphanail, began marketing nail polish exclusively to men. Featuring mixed martial arts fighters as spokesmen, the company tried to portray a hyper-masculine image, claiming that its products would make men more alluring to the opposite sex. Other companies, such as BB Couture, Essie, Manglaze, and EvolutionMan, have all featured "men's" nail polish. While these companies have seen some measure of success, nail polish worn by men still represents a limited niche market.

For More Information

Hoobler, Dorothy, and Thomas Hoobler. *Vanity Rules: A History of American Fashion and Beauty*. Brookfield, CT: Twenty-First Century Books, 2000.

Macedo, Diane. "J.Crew Ad Showing Boy with Pink Nail Polish Sparks Debate on Gender Identity." *Fox News,* April 11, 2011. http://www.foxnews.com/

us/2011/04/11/jcrew-ad-showing-boy-pink-nail-polish-sparks-debate-gender-identity/ (accessed on September 4, 2012).

Nierenberg, Cari. "Athletic Dudes' Girly Little Secret: The Pedi." *Health on TODAY,* April 8, 2012. http://todayhealth.today.msnbc.msn.com/_news/2012/04/08/11061065-athletic-dudes-girly-little-secret-the-pedi?lite (accessed on September 4, 2012).

Patel, Ari. "Alpha Nails: Men's Nail Polish That Gives You 'Swag And Sex.'" *Huffington Post,* March 7, 2012. http://www.huffingtonpost.ca/2012/03/07/alpha-nails-nailpolish-_n_1324982.html#s762175&title=Fighter_Nick_Gonzalez (accessed on September 4, 2012).

Footwear, 1919–29

Shoe and boot styles altered little for men, but a great deal for women, during the 1920s. For everyday occasions men continued to wear either plain or two-toned oxfords with rounded toes, sometimes with spats (linen or canvas shoe coverings) that covered their ankles and the tops of their shoes. As sports became more popular during the decade both men and women wore shoes made especially for sports, like the tennis shoes first popularized in the nineteenth century. Shoes with two colors and fringed tongue flaps became especially popular among men playing golf.

Women's shoe styles became much flashier between 1919 and 1929. As the decade began women wore many plain shoe styles, but one of the most popular was a high-buttoned, high-heeled shoe with a dark leather foot and a contrasting top made to fit closely against the ankle up to mid calf with many small buttons. Some shoes were fastened with as many as sixteen tiny buttons. But as the decade continued, women stopped shunning ornament because rationing and frugality were no longer needed to support World War I (1914–18). Shoe ornaments, including glittering bows, ruffles, and even bug-shaped pins, were sold to spruce up the old styles of shoes, which featured thick, 1- or 2-inch (3- or 5-centimeter) heels and laced or buttoned closures across the top of the foot. But as hemlines rose to the knee by mid-decade, fashion trends emphasized new shoes as important costume accessories. The most significant new shoe was the T-strap sandal, a style that made women's feet look daintier than older styles. Also shoes were no longer somber in color, as they had been during the war. Many were made with bright contrasting colors and decorated with beadwork, fringe, or painted designs. Some companies began to offer shoe dyeing services so that women could change the color of their shoes to match their outfits.

For More Information

Lawlor, Laurie. *Where Will This Shoe Take You?: A Walk Through the History of Footwear*. New York: Walker and Co., 1996.

Pratt, Lucy, and Linda Woolley. *Shoes.* London, England: V&A Publications, 1999.

Thomas, Pauline Weston. "Flapper Fashion 1920s C20th Fashion History" *Fashion-Era.* http://www.fashion-era.com/flapper_fashion_1920s.htm#1920-1930 Shoes (accessed on September 12, 2012).

High-Heeled Shoes

The high-heeled T-strap shoe was thought to be fashionable and sexy. © HULTON-DEUTSCH COLLECTION/HISTORICAL/CORBIS.

As hemlines began to rise by the mid-1920s, the adornment of women's feet became an essential part of a fashionable outfit. High-heeled shoes with low-cut uppers emphasized women's dainty ankles. For the most part high-heeled shoes had 1- or 2-inch (3- or 5-centimeter) chunky heels. At the beginning of the decade the uppers fastened to the foot with laces or straps with buttons on one side. As the decade continued, the ornamentation on these shoes became fancier and many shoes were designed to match whole outfits.

By mid-decade the T-strap sandal showed off even more of a woman's foot. Like other shoe styles, the T-strap sandal had high heels, but the upper portion of the shoe was cut away into a T-shape to expose the top of the foot. Considered fashionable, if a bit racy, in the 1920s the T-strap sandal became especially popular into the following decade.

SEE ALSO *Volume 4, 1919–29: T-Strap Sandal*

For More Information

Lawlor, Laurie. *Where Will This Shoe Take You?: A Walk Through the History of Footwear*. New York: Walker and Co., 1996.

O'Keeffe, Linda. *Shoes: A Celebration of Pumps, Sandals, Slippers & More.* New York: Workman Publishing Company, 1996.

Pratt, Lucy, and Linda Woolley. *Shoes.* London, England: V&A Publications, 1999.

Spats

Spats are linen or canvas shoe coverings that fasten under the bottom of the shoe and button up the side. They were first designed to protect shoes and ankles from mud and water while walking. However, between 1910 and the mid-1930s, spats eventually became an elegant men's fashion accessory, often associated with gangsters and dandies, a term to describe well-dressed men of the time.

Spats originated in the seventeenth century as leather or cloth coverings called gaiters. Gaiters were leggings that covered the shoe and leg up to the knee. They were worn by both women, whose dresses did little to protect shoes and stockings from mud and water splashes, and men, who at that time wore breeches, a type of pants that ended just below the knee. By the 1700s several European nations had made gaiters a part of their military uniform. Gaiters were also called spatterdash because they protected their wearer from spatters and dashes of muddy water in the street.

Spatterdash, or spats, as they came to be called, remained popular for both men and women for several centuries. During the early part of the 1900s men wore them less frequently, as boots had come into fashion. However, by 1910 shoes were back in style for men, and a kind of shortened spat became a required part of the wardrobe of the well-to-do male, giving a "boot look" to shoes. The new spats were made in the era's fashionable colors, which had names like dove (gray) and biscuit (off-white), and were made of heavy canvas in the winter and linen in the summer. A line of pearl buttons often fastened the spats at the side. Many men wore spats with a tailored vest, which became known as the Boulevard Style.

Spats were originally designed to protect shoes, but they became a fashion statement among elegant men and, later, gangsters. © DANI SIMMONDS/ SHUTTERSTOCK.COM.

Spats became a part of gangsters' wardrobes during the 1920s. In January 1920 a law called Prohibition was passed forbidding the sale of alcoholic beverages. This caused a tremendous rise in the illegal manufacture and sale of alcohol, and the rise of the gangster, a member of a gang of criminals. Gangsters were often wealthy and dressed in expensive, stylish, and flamboyant clothes. The clothes worn by gangsters influenced fashions in the United States and Europe from the 1920s through the 1940s. White or gray spats became almost as identified with the gangster as his machine gun, and many men copied the style of the gangsters and the movie stars who played gangsters.

By the mid-1940s spats had, for the most part, disappeared from the fashion scene, replaced by rubber galoshes, which did a much better job of keeping feet warm and dry. During the 1990s, however, spats made a brief comeback as designer fashion accessories for both women and men. Outside the realm of mainstream fashion, spats remain as a part of certain uniforms, most notably the Royal Regiment of Scotland, whose kilted ceremonial uniforms also call for white gaiters to be worn over their shoes. Many marching bands and pipe bands around the world also continue to wear spats on parade.

For More Information

The Royal Regiment of Scotland. "The Royal Regiment of Scotland Dress Regulations." http://www.scribd.com/doc/22636965/The-Royal-Regiments-of-Scotland-Dress-Regulations (accessed on September 4, 2012).

Schoeffler, O. E., and William Gale. *Esquire's Encyclopedia of 20th Century Men's Fashions.* New York: McGraw-Hill, 1973.

T-Strap Sandal

The women's T-strap sandal was first popularized during the 1920s as women began to show off more of their legs and feet. The style featured a pointed toe with a strap that reached toward the ankle from the center of the toe to a horizontal strap circling the ankle. The style covered just the woman's heel and toes but otherwise showed a great deal of the foot, in keeping with the revealing styles of the time. Typically the shoes had a 1- to 2-inch (3- to 5-centimeter) heel. The T-strap was one of the more popular styles for evening wear in the 1930s and early 1940s. However, by the mid-1930s the toe of the shoe became more rounded and the heel lowered, and by the mid-1940s the simple pump was preferred.

For More Information

Mulvagh, Jane. *Vogue History of 20th Century Fashion*. New York: Viking, 1988.

Pratt, Lucy, and Linda Woolley. *Shoes*. London, England: V&A Publications, 1999.

Wing Tips

Wing tips are men's lace-up oxford shoes that are designed with a decorative leather cap on the toe, which is cut in a "winged" design. The cap usually also has other ornamental touches, such as patterns of holes cut or pressed into the leather. First designed in the early 1900s as a high-heeled dress shoe with a wide bow, wing tips have remained as a fashionable lace-up shoe for men into the twenty-first century.

While boots had been the fashionable footwear for men at the end of the 1800s and the beginning of the 1900s, by 1910 shoes returned to favor. By the 1920s male footwear was not only functional but also quite colorful and stylish. A new "cap toe" shoe came into fashion, which had a second layer of covering at the end of the toe, partly for protection and partly for decoration. The wing tip was an elaboration on the straight cap toe design. Where the original cap had been cut straight across the toe of the shoe, the wing tip was cut into a scalloped shape, with a point in the center. The cap was then decorated with holes and designs stamped into it. Many flashy wing tips of the 1920s were two-toned, with the body of the shoe white and the cap and heel either brown or black. Two-toned wing tips were called "spectator shoes," and some fashion historians think that their design was an imitation of the popular spats, a protective cloth garment that covered the shoe from toe to heel. Sporty wing tips sometimes had a fringed flap of leather that covered the shoelaces.

Though wing tips began as part of fashionable young men's wardrobes during the Roaring Twenties, the period of time following World

Wing tips, once a staple in young men's wardrobes, later came to be associated with conservative businessmen. © PBNJ PRODUCTIONS/CORBIS BRIDGE/ALAMY.

War I (1914–18) when Americans were experiencing a newfound freedom and sense of rebellion, they soon became one of the most popular conservative shoe styles for men, who wore them not only as dress shoes but also as part of a middle-class business uniform. Wing tips have remained the preferred style of business executives, lawyers, and other male professionals into the twenty-first century. In fact wing tips are so identified with white-collar males that the shoe has come to represent the corporate world. In headlines such as "The Gumshoe Gets Wing-tips: Private-Investigator Business Takes on Corporate Identity" from the *Washington Post* in 1997 and "Generals Trade Their Army Boots for Wingtips in Trek to Civilian Jobs" from a 1996 article in the *Christian Science Monitor,* it is generally understood that putting on wing tips means entering the business world.

For More Information

Schoeffler, O. E., and William Gale. *Esquire's Encyclopedia of 20th Century Men's Fashions.* New York: McGraw-Hill, 1973.

Difficult Years: 1930–45

Few people living in the booming 1920s could have predicted that the fifteen-year period starting in 1930 would be one of the most difficult times of the entire twentieth century. Yet these fifteen years are now so closely associated with two sustained historical events, the Great Depression (1929–39) and World War II (1939–45), it might seem that little else mattered during these years. Those events gripped the entire world, with ten years of economic hardship capped by six years of a bloody war that touched nearly every part of the globe. Given these important events, it is hard to remember that the 1930s and early 1940s also were a time of real innovations in popular culture, technology, and government. Both the difficulties and the triumphs of this period were reflected in the fashions of the time.

The Great Depression

In late October 1929 the world's largest stock market, the New York Stock Exchange, endured its biggest crash, or decline in the value of stocks, in history. This crash ended what had been a sustained boom in the economies of the United States, the world's most powerful country, and the rest of the Western world. What began as a simple dip in stock prices soon grew much worse, as the world's economies spiraled downward into what would be the worst economic depression in modern history. Factories closed, people lost their jobs and homes, and millions of people grew desperate. Many even faced starvation. As the economic troubles endured for year after year, this time became known as the Great Depression.

The Depression affected the United States and Europe quite differently. The situation was desperate in the United States, where thirteen million people were unemployed and a terrible drought in the nation's agricultural area reduced food supplies and drove thousands off their land, yet the people of the United States came together to combat

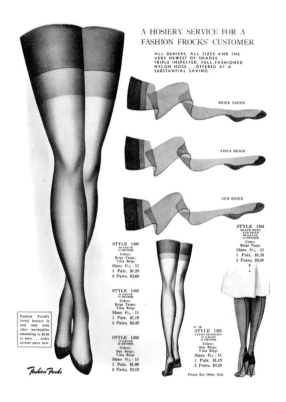

A HOSIERY SERVICE FOR A
FASHION FROCKS' CUSTOMER

ALL DENIERS, ALL SIZES AND THE
VERY NEWEST OF SHADES...
TRIPLE INSPECTED, FULL-FASHIONED
NYLON HOSE...OFFERED AT A
SUBSTANTIAL SAVING.

BEIGE TAUPE

VISTA BEIGE

SUN BEIGE

STYLE 1491
40 GAUGE
15 DENIER
Colors:
Beige Taupe;
Vista Beige
Sizes 8½ - 11
1 Pair, $1.29
3 Pairs, $3.69

STYLE 1492
51 GAUGE
15 DENIER
Colors:
Beige Taupe;
Vista Beige
Sizes 8½ - 11
1 Pair, $1.19
3 Pairs, $3.49

STYLE 1493
45 GAUGE
30 DENIER
Colors:
Sun Beige;
Vista Beige
Sizes 8½ - 11
1 Pair, $1.09
3 Pairs, $3.19

STYLE 1494
BLACK HEEL
AND SEAM
40 GAUGE
15 DENIER
Color:
Beige Taupe
Sizes 8½ - 11
1 Pair, $1.39
3 Pairs, $3.98

STYLE 1495
NYLON SEAMLESS
51 GAUGE
15 DENIER
Colors:
Sun Beige;
Vista Beige
Sizes 8½ - 11
1 Pair, $1.19
3 Pairs, $3.49

Please See Other Side

Fashion Frock's
lovely hosiery is
sold only with
other merchandise
amounting to $2.98
or more ... order
several pairs now.

An advertisement for the newly invented nylon stockings. Following World War I, many young people rejected the modesty of the older generation and embraced all that was new and exciting. © BUYENLARGE/ ARCHIVE PHOTOS/GETTY IMAGES.

the Depression. The government of President Franklin D. Roosevelt (1882–1945) created a set of programs, known as the New Deal, that helped protect people from the worst effects of the Depression and provided jobs for millions. The New Deal greatly expanded the power of government, which many found disturbing, but it is widely credited with helping the United States avoid the internal turmoil that tore Europe apart.

Trouble in Europe leads to war

The economies of Europe were closely tied to the United States, and the Depression that began in the United States soon hit Europe as well. European politicians failed to devise programs to guide their countries safely through the Depression. Instead, Europe's major powers fell back on the habits of mistrust and blame that had led them into war in the past, most recently World War I (1914–18). In Germany especially, resentments over the way their country had been treated after World War I helped fuel the rise of the Nazi Party, a party led by Adolf Hitler (1889–1945) that favored a strong, military government and was based in extreme national pride as well as racism and anti-Semitism, or hatred toward Jews. Hitler blamed other countries and Jewish people for the troubles in his country. He convinced the German people to follow him in his desperate quest to conquer the world, and in 1939 he began to invade the neighboring countries of Poland and Czechoslovakia.

Germany's aggression in 1939 soon brought the other major European powers, Great Britain and France, into the war. Just as in World War I, the conflict soon drew in the rest of the world. Russia soon joined with Britain and France. Allying itself with Germany, Japan tried to seize power in eastern Asia, and it attacked the United States at Pearl Harbor, in Hawaii, in 1941. Soon the United States entered the war as well, on the side of the British, French, and Russians. Many other countries also became involved.

For nearly six years countries fought in bloody battles across Europe, in the Pacific, and in Africa. Millions died and millions more were driven from their homes. Entire countries directed their efforts to winning the war, building ships, tanks, planes, and guns. These efforts ended the economic decline that had gripped the world through the 1930s. Finally in 1945 the Germans were defeated in Europe and the United States dropped two atomic bombs on Japan, forcing the Japanese to surrender. There was no simple way to count the costs or assess the benefits of victory in this disastrous conflict, though the victorious countries prided themselves on having defeated the evil dictator Adolf Hitler and made the world safe for democracy.

A silver lining

It is tempting to view the 1930s and early 1940s in entirely negative terms, defined as they are by depression and war. Yet there were real elements of hope and progress throughout this period. In the United States especially, popular entertainment flowered as never before as people were looking for things to take their minds off their troubles. The 1930s were Hollywood's Golden Age, and motion picture studios produced some of their most interesting and entertaining films of all time. Hollywood stars and starlets came to be the era's greatest celebrities and some of its most important fashion trendsetters. The popularity of sports also grew, with boxing and baseball leading the way. American musicians grew more confident and creative; composers such as Aaron Copland (1900–1990) and George Gershwin (1898–1937) gained international fame, and jazz music grew more sophisticated and interesting. The 1930s also saw the birth of detective novels and comic books.

Other advances of the period also are worthy to note. In medicine, advances in medication allowed for much more effective treatment of infectious diseases, and the development of X-rays revolutionized the way doctors viewed the human body. Technological innovations brought the world faster airplanes and trains, bigger dams that allowed for the creation of more electricity, taller skyscrapers, and—with tragic consequences—bigger and more powerful weapons of destruction. The year 1939 also saw the introduction of the device that would change entertainment in the second half of the twentieth century: the television.

For the very wealthy, the 1930s were a liberating, energizing time. While the masses struggled, the rich enjoyed fancy cars and

Hollywood Influences Fashion

During the 1920s and 1930s, with the rise in popularity of Hollywood movies, screen idols became role models for the masses. Most major fashion trends no longer were dictated only by the top Paris-based fashion houses. The clothes and hairstyles worn by glamorous movie stars, both on and off the screen, grabbed the attention of American and European moviegoers and launched countless fashion fads.

The influence of Hollywood on fashion began during the silent film era, which ended in the late 1920s. Pola Negri (c. 1894–1987), a popular actress of the 1920s, purchased white satin shoes that she had dyed to match her outfits. Once this was publicized, women by the thousands followed her lead. Clara Bow (1905–1965), another silent screen star, helped to popularize bobbed hair, sailor pants, and pleated skirts. Gloria Swanson (1899–1983) made fashionable high-heeled shoes decorated with imitation pearls and rhinestones.

Hollywood costume designers played a crucial role in dictating fashion trends. Between 1928 and 1941, Gilbert Adrian (1903–1959) headed the costume department at Metro-Goldwyn-Mayer (MGM), then the most prestigious Hollywood movie studio. Not only did Adrian create the signature styles of the studio's top actresses, but he launched various fashion crazes. One was the popularity of the gingham dress, a cotton fabric dress featuring a checked or striped pattern, which he designed for Judy Garland (1922–1969) to wear in *The Wizard of Oz* (1939) and for Katharine Hepburn (1907–2003) in *The Philadelphia Story* (1940). Another famous Hollywood designer was Hubert de Givenchy (1927–), who was a favorite of influential actress Audrey Hepburn and dressed her in such movies as *Breakfast at Tiffany's* (1961), *Sabrina* (1954), and *Funny Face* (1957).

Actress Audrey Hepburn wearing a gown by Hubert de Givenchy. © BETTMANN/HISTORICAL/CORBIS.

yachts, travel, and rich clothes and accessories. Wealthy women traveled to Paris, France, and gladly paid thousands of dollars for dresses designed by prestigious designers. Wealthy men flocked to Savile Row in London, England, to have their suits custom made. Both men and women

Outfits worn in movies were quickly copied by retailers. A woman who found a dress or gown worn in a movie appealing could purchase a low-priced copy in a department store or from a Sears catalog. Magazines published clothing patterns based on film costumes, allowing women to sew their own Hollywood-style frocks. The era's most favored pattern reportedly was a dress worn by Vivien Leigh (1913–1967) in a picnic scene in *Gone with the Wind* (1939), one of the era's most popular and publicized movies.

Individual performers became associated with clothes or hairstyles that became their trademarks. In the early 1930s sultry Jean Harlow (1911–1937) was famed for her platinum blonde hair, which was a very light, almost-white blonde color. In fact, *Platinum Blonde* (1931) was the title of one of her early film successes. The platinum blonde effect was achieved by bleaching the hair. When Harlow ascended to stardom, women began coloring their hair in order to copy her look. In the 1940s Veronica Lake (1919–1973), a rising star, launched a trend by wearing her hair in peek-a-boo bangs, with her long blonde locks falling over one eye. Dorothy Lamour (1914–1996) popularized the sarong, a one-piece, wrap-around garment worn primarily as a skirt or dress, when she played the exotically beautiful title character in *The Jungle Princess* (1936).

If Harlow, Lake, and Lamour represented sex appeal, child star Shirley Temple (1928–) personified sweetness and innocence. During the mid-1930s Temple enjoyed a run as the movie industry's number-one box office star. Mothers dressed their daughters like Temple and styled their hair to copy her trademark ringlet curls. No little girl's toy chest was complete without a Shirley Temple doll, of which more than six million were sold. Meanwhile, the great popularity of cowboy movies, particularly among the young, hiked the sales of western-style shirts for adults as well as children.

Katharine Hepburn, Greta Garbo (1905–1990), and Marlene Dietrich (c. 1901–1992) were strong-willed personalities, both on and off the screen. Each preferred wearing trousers at a time when females were expected to convey their womanliness by donning dresses and skirts. Hepburn's, Garbo's, and Dietrich's choice of attire communicated to women that they neither would squander away their femininity nor be any less appealing to men if they chose pants over dresses.

Occasionally what stars chose not to wear had a major impact on fashion trends. In the early 1930s men commonly wore undershirts. Then Clark Gable (1901–1960), one of the era's top stars and most influential male icons, appeared in *It Happened One Night* (1934). At one point in the film Gable brashly removes his shirt, revealing his bare chest. He was not wearing an undershirt. After the release of *It Happened One Night,* undershirt sales across the United States plummeted by a reported 75 percent. Films and film stars continue to influence fashion trends to the present day.

increasingly wore looser, more comfortable clothes for their daily activities, pioneering the idea of leisure clothes. Though their fashion choices were beyond the reach of the vast majority of people, the tastes of the rich filtered down into the fashions of the 1930s and early 1940s.

For More Information

Feinstein, Stephen. *The 1930s: From the Great Depression to the Wizard of Oz.* Berkeley Heights, NJ: Enslow, 2001.

Feinstein, Stephen. *The 1940s: From World War II to Jackie Robinson.* Berkeley Heights, NJ: Enslow, 2000.

Hills, Ken. *The 1940s.* Austin, TX: Raintree Steck-Vaugh, 1992.

Press, Petra. *The 1930s.* San Diego, CA: Lucent, 1999.

Schraff, Anne E. *The Great Depression and the New Deal: America's Economic Collapse and Recovery.* New York: F. Watts, 1990.

"The Great Depression." *History.com.* http://www.history.com/topics/great-depression (accessed on September 12, 2012).

Clothing, 1930–45

When it comes to fashion, the 1930s was a complex age. On the one hand, fashions were deeply influenced by the economic depression that gripped the Western world throughout the 1930s; on the other hand, fashions in the 1930s were very elegant, with clothing trends largely determined by the tastes of the very wealthy, especially movie stars and other celebrities. Strangely, these two influences came together to create clothing styles that were simple yet elegant. The coming of World War II in 1939 brought a completely new set of pressures to the way people dressed, with rationing (limiting) of clothing, government dress codes, and the German occupation of Paris, France, the world's fashion capital, altering clothing styles dramatically.

Clothing and the Great Depression

The 1930s began with a dramatic shift in the overall silhouette, or shape, of clothing for both men and women. Reacting against the trends of the 1920s, both men's and women's clothing became sleeker and more streamlined. Women's hemlines extended down the leg and both men's and women's clothing accented simple, flowing lines. Leading the way in these changes were designers from Paris, actors and actresses from Hollywood, and wealthy socialites from around the world. The leading designers of the day, all based in Paris, included Gabrielle "Coco" Chanel (1883–1971), Elsa Schiaparelli (1890–1973), and Madeleine Vionnet (1876–1975). Schiaparelli was especially famous for her adventurous experiments with new fabrics, patterns, and wild colors. Her introduction

Nazi Style

Every nation that fought in World War II (1939–45) created standardized uniforms for their soldiers. The most dramatic uniforms were worn by the Nazi soldiers of the German army. With their mania for black leather, brass buttons, medals, and armbands, the Nazis proved as bold in their fashions as they were brutal on the battlefield. The German uniform style during the Nazi period was so eccentric that the American novelist Kurt Vonnegut (1922–) called it "madly theatrical."

After seizing power in Germany in 1933 under the leadership of Adolf Hitler (1889–1945), the Nazi Party put in place a totalitarian state (a strictly controlled state under the leadership of a dictator) that left no aspect of German society untouched. Uniforms became the norm for both civilian (nonmilitary) and military dress. But where other totalitarian societies, such as Russia, opted for functional dress codes and muted color schemes that de-emphasized individuality, the Nazis preferred expressive styles designed to make the ordinary citizen feel like part of a grand-national enterprise. The development of smart-looking uniforms for everybody provided visible evidence of German unity.

Nowhere was this sense of identity more evident than in the German military. The Nazis believed that their army represented a modern recreation of the Teutonic (or ancient German) Knights, the mysterious military order of medieval Europe. Instead of the chain mail (armor made of interlinking metal rings) and plate armor the knights would have worn, the Nazis substituted black leather. The Gestapo, Nazi Germany's secret police force, called attention to itself by wearing black fedora hats and ankle-length black leather trench coats. The brutal S.S. Panzer military divisions struck fear in the hearts of their adversaries with black forage caps (caps commonly worn by soldiers during the American Civil War [1861–65] with visors of roughly cut pieces of leather that rapidly assumed a curved shape and sides that collapsed so the top tended to incline forward), jump boots, and stylish black leather jackets. (A few decades later Western teenage "rockers" could be seen sporting virtually the same ensemble.)

of a bold pink was so shocking that it helped coin the term "shocking pink." Hollywood stars and starlets like Gary Cooper (1901–1961) and Marlene Dietrich (c. 1901–1992) made fashion news with their bold fashion choices; Cooper became associated with the English drape suit for men and Dietrich with the pants suit for women. Finally, wealthy jet-setters turned sports clothing into daily wear, introducing such items as the knit polo shirt into common usage.

The bold experiments and new styles introduced by the wealthy were out of reach for most people, as the period of great economic turmoil known as the Great Depression (1929–39) put many out of work and reduced the incomes of most people. Yet several trends combined to

Though Nazis were defeated in World War II, their style of dress—leather jackets, thick-soled boots—lives on.
© STUART NICOL/HULTON ARCHIVE/GETTY IMAGES.

Variations on this same dark outfit also were adopted by German fighter pilots and undersea U-boat crews. No one in the Nazi high command, not even Adolf Hitler himself, felt fully equipped without an extensive leather wardrobe.

After Germany's defeat by the Allied powers, including the United States, Great Britain, Russia, and their allies, in 1945, the Nazi regime was destroyed, but its style lingered on in movies and in television shows. One of the common elements of Nazi dress, the black leather jacket, became a popular symbol of rebellion that was worn by rock 'n' rollers in the 1950s and beyond. The popular heavy black boots known as Dr. Martens also closely resemble Nazi jump boots. One of the most important symbols of Nazi style, the swastika, has remained off limits to fashion's reinterpretation and reuse, for it is too closely associated with the horror of Nazi rule, especially the mass extermination of Jews in German death camps. This symbol remains illegal in Germany and Austria, and in the rest of Europe it is universally shunned. However, some modern militant groups, including skinheads and Neo-Nazis, display such socially unacceptable symbols as a form of protest, even tattooing the swastika on themselves to show their allegiance to the Nazi ideals.

allow common people to enjoy the new fashions despite the hard times. The newer fashions didn't use a great deal of fabric, so people could make their own clothes with less fabric and thus less cost. Especially in the United States, the ready-to-wear clothing industry had advanced in its ability to produce and sell inexpensively a wide range of sizes and styles. Clothing manufacturers copied the latest fashions coming out of Paris and produced cheap imitations. They took advantage of inexpensive fabrics like cotton and rayon, which were well-suited to the flowing lines that were so popular. Finally, most people saved money simply by making their clothes last longer. People ignored rapid shifts in fashion and wore the same dresses and suits for several years.

World War II disrupts fashion

The coming of war, first to Europe and soon to virtually the entire world, brought immense changes to the nature of fashion. The world of high fashion was changed most dramatically by the German invasion of France and the occupation of Paris. Most of the great fashion houses that had determined the styles worn in the West were closed; designers fled the country and the wealthy had to look elsewhere for their clothes. Designers in other countries, especially the United States, soon filled the void. Among the many American designers who gained valuable experience and clients during the war years were Mainbocher (1891–1976) and Claire McCardell (1905–1958), who created what became known as the American Look.

The clothing worn by common people also was impacted by the war. Military demands for fabric, especially for use in uniforms, tents, and parachutes, meant that many countries used some form of rationing or limiting fabric and clothing. Clothes makers altered the styles of clothes they made in order to use less fabric: hemlines became shorter, trousers and skirts were closer fitting, and fabric-wasting flourishes such as patch pockets disappeared. The impact of fabric shortages was greatest in Great Britain, where severe limits were set on the amount of clothes or fabric that could be purchased. The British government created a kind of national dress code called utility clothing. Overall, staying in fashion just didn't seem so important during wartime and people didn't mind dressing in simpler, less unique clothes. The war did have one positive impact on fashion: Clothes makers who shifted their work to produce military uniforms became very skilled at producing huge numbers of clothes at a low price. After the war clothing prices fell and quality clothes became available to more people than ever before.

The Depression and World War II were the biggest influences on clothing in the years between 1930 and 1945, but they weren't the only influences. Jazz music, the popularity of sports and sports clothes, and trends in art and industrial design all made an impact.

For More Information

Baker, Patricia. *Fashions of a Decade: The 1940s*. New York: Facts on File, 1992.

Costantino, Maria. *Fashions of a Decade: The 1930s*. New York: Facts on File, 1992.

Dorner, Jane. *Fashion in the Forties and Fifties*. London, England: Ian Allan Ltd., 1973.

Dorner, Jane. *Fashion in the Twenties and Thirties.* London, England: Ian Allan Ltd., 1973.

Ewing, Elizabeth. *History of Twentieth Century Fashion.* Revised by Alice Mackrell. Lanham, MD: Barnes and Noble Books, 1992.

Laver, James. *Costume and Fashion: A Concise History.* 4th ed. London, England: Thames and Hudson, 2002.

Mulvagh, Jane. *Vogue History of 20th Century Fashion.* New York: Viking, 1988.

Payne, Blanche, Geitel Winakor, and Jane Farrell-Beck. *The History of Costume.* 2nd ed. New York: HarperCollins, 1992.

Schoeffler, O. E., and William Gale. *Esquire's Encyclopedia of 20th Century Men's Fashions.* New York: McGraw-Hill, 1973.

Dolman Sleeves

Dolman sleeves, sometimes called batwing sleeves, are sleeves that are cut deep and wide at the shoulder, with armholes extending almost to the waist. The sleeves taper to the wrist, and when the arms are held outward the fabric hangs in a long wing. Unlike set-in sleeves, dolman sleeves are usually cut as one piece with the top of a dress, blouse, jacket, or coat. Full and roomy, the sweeping sleeve had been used for women's clothing since around 1910 but reached a peak of popularity in the early 1940s.

The dolman sleeve design was originally borrowed from a garment worn in Turkey and other parts of the Middle East called a dolman as early as the Middle Ages (c. 500–c. 1500). The dolman was a loose, cape-like robe with very loose sleeves formed from folds of the robe's fabric. Europeans adopted Eastern styles starting in the sixteenth century and used the dolman as a model for a military jacket, also called a dolman, that continues to be worn in parts of Europe in the twenty-first century. The dolman sleeve was simpler to sew than a set-in sleeve, and so it was widely used when sewing techniques were still in the early stages of development.

During the first two decades of the 1900s, people were fascinated by designs from the East,

An illustration showing a woman wearing a dress suit with dolman sleeves. © PARIS PIERCE/ALAMY.

and so the dolman sleeve was revived as a modern, exotic fashion. One of the great appeals of the dolman design is that it gave an elegant, flowing line, while allowing the wearer freedom of movement. In the 1940s, following the hardships of the economic depression of the 1930s, glamour and elegance became very fashionable. The dramatic lines of the dolman sleeve were perfect for those who wanted to dress with the flair and grace of a movie star. In 1941 the dolman dress became one of the most stylish dresses a woman could own.

Within a year, however, World War II (1939–45) had caused fabric shortages throughout Europe and later the United States, and the baggy fabric of the dolman sleeve went out of style. The dolman sleeve returned at the end of the war as part of the ultra-feminine New Look of the late 1940s and early 1950s. The dolman sleeve had another period of high popularity during the 1980s, when it returned as the batwing sleeve, both on formal clothes and on sportswear. In the early twenty-first century, dolman-sleeved tops were commonly available from many ready-to-wear fashion retailers.

For More Information

Baker, Patricia. *Fashions of a Decade: The 1940s*. New York: Facts on File, 1992.

Payne, Blanche, Geitel Winakor, and Jane Farrell-Beck. *The History of Costume.* 2nd ed. New York: HarperCollins, 1992.

Little Black Dress

Introduced in the late 1920s and first popular in the 1930s, the little black dress—a slim-fitting dress of varying length worn for dinners, cocktail parties, and evenings out—was one of the most popular fashions of the twentieth century. Along with blue jeans and the T-shirt, it is one of the most influential and important garments of the twentieth century.

The little black dress made its debut in May 1926, with a pen and ink drawing in *Vogue* magazine by designer Gabrielle "Coco" Chanel (1883–1971). The magazine editors called the dress "Chanel's 'Ford,'" comparing the dress to the simply designed, economically priced black Ford Model T automobile.

The dress caused an instant uproar in the fashion world. Choosing black as a fashionable color was itself startling. Before Chanel, black clothing was associated with either the clergy or servants, or with mourning. But the simplicity and economy of the dress appealed to women of the 1930s Great Depression era, a time of severe economic turmoil after the stock market crash of 1929. With this simple item in their wardrobes, accessorized only with a string of pearls or a pair of high heels, middle-class women and high-society ladies could be equals. As Chanel said, "Thanks to me they [the nonwealthy] can walk around like millionaires."

One of the first celebrities to popularize the little black dress was the cartoon character Betty Boop, the squeaky-voiced, well-proportioned creation of animator Max Fleischer (1883–1972). Wallis Simpson (1896–1986), the American who married the former king of England in 1937, also wore the dress and reportedly said, "When the little black dress is right, there is nothing else to wear in its place," as quoted by Valerie Mendes.

The woman who, according to expert Amy Holman Edelman, "made the little black dress an art form," was actress Audrey Hepburn (1929–1993). She wore a little black dress designed by Hubert de Givenchy (1927–) in the role of free-spirited Holly Golightly in the 1961 film *Breakfast at Tiffany's.*

By the end of the twentieth century almost every major designer from Ralph Lauren (1939–) to Donna Karan (1948–) had included a little black dress in their clothing lines. Amy Holman Edelman, who devoted an entire book, *The Little Black Dress,* to Chanel's creation, has called the dress "emblematic of a woman's freedom of choice, her equal participating in the world and her declaration that, this time, she is dressing for herself."

In the early 2010s, the revolutionary, Paris-based avant-garde designer Rad Hourani shocked, but also thrilled, the mainstream fashion world with his androgynous designs that were meant to be worn by either men or women. His collections have included several unisex variations on the little black dress and were featured on fashion runways, worn by both men and women. Like many other designers, Hourani was inspired by Chanel's revolutionary 1926 creation, especially for using black, his favorite color, to create a modern, popular wardrobe.

For More Information

Costantino, Maria. *Fashions of a Decade: The 1930s.* New York: Facts on File, 1992.

Edelman, Amy Holman. *The Little Black Dress.* New York: Simon and Schuster, 1997.

Haedrich, Marcel. *Coco Chanel: Her Life, Her Secrets.* Boston, MA: Little, Brown, 1971.

Hourani, Rad. "Black Is the New Black." *New York Times,* April 2, 2010. http://tmagazine.blogs.nytimes.com/2010/04/02/black-is-the-new-black/ (accessed on September 4, 2012).

Mendes, Valerie D. *Dressed in Black.* New York: Harry N. Abrams, 1999.

Simon, Francesca. "Emerging Designer Rad Hourani." *iFashion Network,* January 26, 2010. http://www.ifashionnetwork.com/ifashion-designers/idesigner/25-emerging-designers/303-emerging-designer-rad-hourani.html (accessed on September 4, 2012).

Men's Suits

Despite the negative impact of the Great Depression (1929–39), a period of severe economic turmoil that lasted throughout the 1930s, this period is thought of as one of the century's high points in men's suits. Perhaps as a way of rising above the money woes that troubled most people, the very wealthy and the very famous, especially male movie stars, chose beautifully tailored suits made of expensive fabrics. Wealthy gangsters, like Al Capone and Bugs Moran, who became a focus of public attention in the United States during the 1930s, also chose expensive suits. While common men couldn't afford such luxuries, they could buy suits that were modeled after the new styles.

The suit, of course, was the basic uniform of the well-dressed American male, both at work and for nightlife. The basic suit consisted of a jacket and trousers made of matching material; the three-piece suit also had a matching vest, or waistcoat. Both types of suits were worn throughout the Western world and, increasingly, in other parts of the world, such as Japan and China. The basic silhouette, or shape, of the men's suit remained the same throughout the 1930s and featured broad shoulders, a narrowed waist, and loose-fitting, cuffed trousers. By the mid-1940s wartime restrictions called for men's suits to use less fabric, and suits became more closely fitted with no patch pockets or cuffs.

Tailors in London, England, especially those located in the city's famous Savile Row fashion district, set the standard for men's suits, and they popularized the best-known suit of the 1930s, the English drape. With wide, unpadded shoulders and a full-cut chest tapering to a slim waist, the jacket made men look strong. The trousers were cut very full and hung straight from the waist to the cuffed hem. Trousers were worn so high on the waist that belts would not work, so most men held their trousers in place with suspenders, or, as the English called them, braces. The most popular fabric for men's suits was wool, and weaves with a twill or a herringbone (a weave that creates rows of parallel lines sloping in opposite directions) pattern were very common.

A striking contrast to the English drape suit was the glen plaid suit, another product of Great Britain. Glen plaid was the name of the fabric used to make the suit, and it was a boldly patterned plaid, a checkered pattern. The suit was first worn by Britain's Prince of Wales in 1923, but it became popular among college students in the 1930s.

Up until the mid-1930s men tended to wear the same suits year-round, even though wool was often hot and heavy during the summer months. Beginning in the mid-1930s, however, tailors and clothes makers introduced the summer-weight suit. Tropical worsted, a lightweight wool, rayon, or silk, were used, and they cut a suit's weight nearly in half. Most summer suits were worn without a vest.

No matter what suit a man wore, it was always accompanied by a carefully chosen hat and tie. Some men also wore a creased handkerchief in their breast pocket, and the truly stylish carried a walking stick.

For More Information

Costantino, Maria. *Fashions of a Decade: The 1930s*. New York: Facts on File, 1992.

Keers, Paul. *A Gentleman's Wardrobe: Classic Clothes and the Modern Man*. New York: Harmony Books, 1987.

McEvoy, Anne. *The 1920s and 1930s*. New York: Chelsea House, 2009.

Payne, Blanche, Geitel Winakor, and Jane Farrell-Beck. *The History of Costume*. 2nd ed. New York: HarperCollins, 1992.

Schoeffler, O. E., and William Gale. *Esquire's Encyclopedia of 20th Century Men's Fashions*. New York: McGraw-Hill, 1973.

Military Uniforms and Civilian Dress

Military uniforms exist for nearly the opposite reasons of fashionable civilian, or nonmilitary, clothes. Civilian clothes are intended to express the wearer's individuality, to keep up with current trends in cut and fabric, and generally to be expressive. Military uniforms, on the other hand, are intensely practical. While dress uniforms can still be very attractive and made to look impressive, fatigues (battledress or combat uniforms) are meant to provide protection from the elements, to offer storage for the many items soldiers carry, and to identify combatants in the chaos of war. Despite these vast differences, advances made in the manufacturing of military uniforms had a direct impact on civilian dress during and after World War II (1939–45).

As first the major European countries and then the United States entered the war, they each found it necessary to clothe thousands and thousands of soldiers in durable, reasonably well-fitting uniforms tailored to the special needs of different kinds of activity. European countries found that their clothing producers were not able to keep up with demand. Most clothing makers made hundreds of batches of clothes, but the military needed thousands. Standards for determining sizes and for determining what it cost to make an item were very rough.

Though designed to protect and identify soldiers, military uniforms came to have an enormous impact on the manufacturing of civilian clothing. © PLANET NEWS ARCHIVE/SSPL/GETTY IMAGES.

In the United States, however, clothing manufacturers had become very skilled at making ready-to-wear clothes in the 1920s and 1930s. Feeding the large American market, they had learned how to make huge numbers of well-fitting clothes at competitive prices. When the United States entered the war in 1941 these manufacturers stepped in to make uniforms for American soldiers. The United States also sent teams of clothing experts to Britain to help their allies employ better manufacturing methods. American skill and productivity at making all manner of war supplies, including uniforms, surprised the world and was one of the keys to eventual victory in the war.

The skills gained in producing military uniforms had a direct impact on the manufacture of civilian clothing after the war. Clothing makers had learned how to make many thousands of a single item at a low price, and they improved the quality and sizing of the garments they produced. As fabric supplies gradually returned to normal after the war, clothing manufacturers in Europe and the United States were able to offer a steady supply of comfortable ready-to-wear clothes to consumers eager for new products. The quality of these garments narrowed the gap between the clothes worn by the wealthy and those worn by the poor, making good clothing available to more people than ever before.

For More Information

Baker, Patricia. *Fashions of a Decade: The 1940s*. New York: Facts on File, 1992.

Darman, Peter. *Uniforms of World War II*. Edison, NJ: Chartwell Books, 1998.

Ewing, Elizabeth. *History of Twentieth Century Fashion*. Revised by Alice Mackrell. Lanham, MD: Barnes and Noble Books, 1992.

Fussell, Paul. *Uniforms: Why We Are What We Wear*. New York: Houghton Mifflin, 2002.

Stanton, Shelby. *U.S. Army Uniforms of World War II*. Mechanicsburg, PA: Stackpole Books, 1991.

Polo Shirt

A polo shirt is a knitted, short-sleeved pullover shirt with a buttoned placket, a small opening at the neckline, and attached collar. Polo shirts were first knit from wool jersey but soon were knit with cotton and other soft materials. The first polo shirts were part of the uniforms worn by polo players on teams in England and the United States starting at the beginning of the nineteenth century. (Polo is a game in which two teams on horseback use long-handled mallets to drive a ball into the opposing team's goal.) By the late 1920s polo shirts became the preferred shirts of golfers, tennis players, and men sailing yachts, who discovered the comfort and the ease of movement such shirts allowed. Tennis player Jean René Lacoste (1904–1996) even started selling his own brand of polo shirt with a crocodile logo embroidered on the chest in honor of his nickname, "Crocodile." As sports increased in popularity into the 1930s, polo shirts became fashionable shirts for men watching sports or just lounging around. No matter the sport or casual affair to which men chose to wear these sporty shirts, the shirts have always been called polo shirts.

Very rich men made the polo shirt fashionable. At the depths of the economical turmoil of the Great Depression (1929–39) new, fashionable clothes were only available to the wealthy. Fashion magazines filled their pages with descriptions and pictures of the outfits worn at fancy vacation spots such as the French Riviera or Palm Beach, Florida. By the mid-1930s the polo shirt was among the most popular leisure shirts for men. *Esquire* magazine reported that navy blue polo shirts had reached the "status of a uniform" on golf courses in 1934, according to O.E. Schoeffler and William Gale in their book *Esquire's Encyclopedia of 20th Century Men's Fashions.* Commonly made of a plain knit material, polo shirts with a herringbone pattern also were favored. The style developed to include versions with buttons down the entire front and some with no buttons, only a V-neck opening at the collar.

When World War II began in 1939 knitted shirts temporarily dropped out of favor and they were hardly seen until the end of the war in 1945. After the war, polo shirts returned to fashion. The most enduring fashion trend polo shirts ushered in was an acceptance of shirts worn without neckwear, which has lasted to the present day.

For More Information

Dorner, Jane. *Fashion in the Forties and Fifties.* London, England: Ian Allan Ltd., 1973.

Dorner, Jane. *Fashion in the Twenties and Thirties.* London, England: Ian Allan Ltd., 1973.

Schoeffler, O. E., and William Gale. *Esquire's Encyclopedia of 20th Century Men's Fashions.* New York: McGraw-Hill, 1973.

Rationing Fashion in the United States

In 1941, upon the United States's entry into World War II (1939–45), the commercial manufacture of many types of clothing ceased for the war's duration. The materials from which clothing was made—including nylon, silk, leather, and rubber—were required for the manufacture of products that were essential to fighting the war. In January 1942 the War Production Board was established by order of President Franklin Roosevelt (1882–1945). The board was charged with changing and expanding the nation's economy to assist in the war effort. Before its abolishment in November 1945, the board administered the production of $185 billion in supplies and weapons. As a result of the war effort, civilians had to make do with unstylish, everyday items of clothing. Women in particular were challenged to work around these restrictions while still making their clothing a reflection of their femininity.

For women, the plight caused by the nylon stocking was a typical wartime dilemma. The first nylon stockings were introduced into the marketplace in 1939 and proved an immediate success. But once the United States went to war in 1941, nylon was needed to produce parachutes and tires, and nylon stockings disappeared from stores. Some women who wished to at least maintain the illusion of style went so far as to paint black seams up the backs of their legs, to create the impression that they were wearing stockings. So scarce were nylon stockings that a single pair, famously worn by pinup model Betty Grable, was auctioned off at a war bond rally for forty thousand dollars. By the end of the war, stores once again began carrying nylon stockings, and women were so keen to purchase them that "nylon riots" took place, in which women in large cities like New York and San Francisco smashed store windows and brawled with each other in an effort to obtain a pair.

Other popular clothing items disappeared, including dresses, blouses, ties, silk underwear, rubber-soled shoes, leather shoes, and handbags. Leather shoes were replaced by those made of canvas, mesh, and reptile skin; elevated wood and cork soles substituted for leather and rubber soles. Even the more common materials, including wool and cotton, had to be set aside for military uniforms. The War Production Board established guidelines that lessened the amount of fabric that manufacturers could use in the production of civilian clothing by 15 percent.

British Utility Clothing

During World War II (1939–45), as part of their overall effort to involve all citizens in the war effort, the British government declared that all nonmilitary clothing should be simply and plainly designed. Practicality, rather than style, was the rule, and not an extra inch of fabric was to be wasted in the manufacture of clothing. The garments produced under the new rules were called utility clothes, and they first made their way onto the marketplace in 1941.

In order to smooth the progress of the war effort, the British government took control of the import and production of raw materials and provided fabrics to clothing producers. Clothes makers were encouraged to manufacture clothing in a narrow range of styles. Utility garments were like military uniforms in that they were simple and standardized. They even were labeled with a "CC41" insignia, which stood for "Civilian Clothing 1941" or "Clothing Control 1941." To conserve fabric, utility clothing had small pockets and men's pants had no cuffs. Shirt, skirt, and dress lengths were shortened. Garments had no more than three buttons. Shoes were plain and sturdy. Utility clothing prices were controlled to make them affordable to all.

Then in 1942, the British government issued the Civilian Clothing Order, which added the weight of the law to utility styles. Under the order it became illegal to decorate clothing with extra embroidery, buttons, or pockets. Law or no law, ornate clothing designs and accessories had come to be viewed as being in bad taste.

At first, consumers expected to be displeased with utility clothing, which they assumed would be drab and boring. Once the clothing reached stores, however, shoppers realized that utility clothing was durable and, while generally lacking flair and distinctiveness, did come in different styles and colors. In fact, in 1942 members of the Incorporated Society of London Fashion Designers united to create thirty-four utility clothing designs. These were approved by the government, mass-produced, and came with the "CC41" label.

Great Britain was so weakened by the war that clothing rationing had to be maintained until 1949. The utility clothing concept, meanwhile, became such a part of the fabric of British life that it was eventually introduced for furniture as well. Utility clothes remained on the marketplace until 1952, seven full years after the war's end.

Any clothing style that depended upon an excess of fabric was now unpatriotic. Double-breasted (two rows of buttons down the front) suits, double cuffs on shirts, cuffs on trousers, extra pockets on suits, and patch pockets (pockets created by attaching an extra piece of material to a garment) became socially unacceptable. So did full skirts, flowing evening gowns, and wide hems on dresses and skirts.

Civilian clothing became less frequently replaced, and more often was mended when the individual item otherwise might have been discarded. Old items of clothing were reshaped and sewn into new ones.

Even wedding gowns were reused by sisters and friends of the bride and finally were remade into nightgowns or underwear. Fashion magazines published patterns, or clothing designs, that illustrated how men's suits could be altered into women's suits and women's dresses could be transformed into clothing for girls. The government even issued a directive that no more than five thousand dollars could be spent on costumes for each Hollywood movie. To conform to this restriction, moviemakers began recycling costumes from previous films.

Increasing numbers of women took industrial jobs, replacing the men who had gone off to war. Because such feminine apparel as skirts and dresses were impractical on-the-job attire, women began wearing overalls and pants, leading to more women dressing in pants away from work. In fact, pants came to signify the contribution of women to the war effort.

Because of the restrictions of war, people became more imaginative in the ways they used clothing to express their sense of style. Simple black dresses became popular because they easily could be reworn with different colored scarves, bows, and pins. Hairstyles became more ornate and imaginative. Men's clothing even became more casual and vibrant. While not in uniform, a man might sport a brightly patterned tie. Soldiers arriving home from fighting in the Pacific brought with them colorful aloha shirts.

It took nearly two years after the war's end for supplies of fabric and materials to return to normal. In 1947 the legendary fashion designer Christian Dior (1905–1957) introduced his New Look, which spotlighted women's clothing featuring fuller skirts and longer lengths.

SEE ALSO *Volume 4, 1930–45: Little Black Dress; Volume 5, 1946–60: New Look*

For More Information

Baker, Patricia. *Fashions of a Decade: The 1940s.* New York: Facts on File, 1992.

Laboissonniere, Wade. *Blueprints of Fashion: Home Sewing Patterns of the 1940s.* Atglen, PA: Schiffer Publishing, 1997.

Peacock, John. *The 1940s.* New York: Thames and Hudson, 1998.

Russell, Bruce. "Synthetic Wonder." *New Straits Times,* January 17, 1988. http://news.google.com/newspapers?nid=1309&dat=19880117&id=P7BUAAAAIBAJ&sjid=XZADAAAAIBAJ&pg=5411,361405 (accessed on September 4, 2012).

Sladen, Christopher. *The Conscription of Fashion: Utility Cloth, Clothing and Footwear, 1941–1952.* Brookfield, CT: Ashgate Publishing, 1995.

Sarongs

A sarong is a free-fitting garment consisting of a length or tube of cloth that is wrapped around the waist and worn as a skirt. It is worn in many cultures as a part of traditional or ethnic costume. Unlike countries such as Bangladesh, Indonesia, Myanmar, Samoa, and Sri Lanka, where sarongs are very common among men, when the sarong was popularized in the West, it was adopted primarily by women. Sarongs are multicolored and feature an endless array of patterns. When they became popular in the mid-1930s they suggested an exotic, friendly allure.

The striking patterns and colors on traditional sarongs were produced by a method known as batik, a slow and complex process of dying that involves covering the areas of the cloth that are not to be colored with melted wax. The cloth is exposed to the dye or dyes, and then the wax is removed by placing it in boiling water. A sarong made by this two-thousand-year-old process may take well more than a year to produce.

Actress Dorothy Lamour, pictured here, popularized the sarong by wearing them in her role for the film titled Jungle Princess. © POPPERFOTO/ GETTY IMAGES.

In the United States sarongs were popularized in the movies, especially by the popular actress Dorothy Lamour (1914–1996), who won stardom in the mid-1930s and remained a top screen personality throughout the 1940s, often cast as an exotic, sarong-clad island woman. Lamour's star-making role was in *The Jungle Princess* (1936), in which she played Ulah, an exotically beautiful female who grew up alone in the wilds of Malaysia. Lamour actually wore a sarong only in a fraction of her future films, yet her career was forever linked to the garment.

Sarongs were made of cotton or silk and, later, rayon. In addition to skirts and dresses, they have been worn as jackets, sashes, shawls, and head coverings. Sarongs can be folded several different ways and tied with knots before being placed on, over, or around the body. In some parts of the world, sarongs also double as sleeping blankets at night. Sarongs have been used not only to cover the body but also as colorful curtains, window shades, tablecloths, beach or pool towels, wall hangings, and even bandanas for dogs. In the later years of the twentieth century they found increased popularity as a cover worn over swimsuits, and this practice has continued into the twenty-first century.

For More Information

"Men in Sarong: Celebrities and Sexy Male Models." *Famewatcher*, February 6, 2009. http://famewatcher.com/asian-male-fashion-sarong-wrap-for-men-beach-wear.html (accessed on September 4, 2012).

Lamour, Dorothy, as told to Dick McInnes. *My Side of the Road.* Englewood Cliffs, NJ: Prentice Hall, 1980.

Yarwood, Doreen. *The Encyclopedia of World Costume.* New York: Charles Scribner's Sons, 1978.

Stockings

Long used to describe socks or any covering for the feet, the term "stockings" has come to refer to the sheer foot and leg coverings worn mainly by women. Once made of thick cotton or wool, stockings were mostly hidden under long skirts and only seen in provocative glimpses. Since the 1920s, however, women's skirt lengths have remained well above the ankle, and sheer, colored, embroidered, or patterned stockings have become a highly visible fashion accessory. Since the beginning of the 1940s most stockings have been made from nylon.

Knitted stockings have been commonly available since an English clergyman named William Lee (c. 1550–1610) invented a knitting machine in 1589. Though women had worn plain cotton or wool stockings for centuries, it took the rising hemlines of the 1920s to make stockings fashionable. Young women wearing their skirts at knee length wanted to show off their legs in pretty stockings. Soon embroidered cotton stockings appeared, but these became baggy around the knees after a few wearings. Even rayon, a new sheer fabric invented in Germany in 1915, had the same problem. Stockings made of silk held their shape better and soon became quite popular, though they were expensive. Manufacturers began to make stockings in a variety of flesh colors, and soon legs appeared almost bare, except for the seam that ran up the back. Silk stockings were held up by garters, elastic circles that fit tightly around each leg, or garter belts, elastic bands that went around the waist with several fasteners that hung down to secure the stockings.

A woman modeling stockings held up with garters.
© HULTON ARCHIVE/STRINGER/ GETTY IMAGES.

Women preferred silk stockings, but they were easily torn, so in the late 1930s scientists at the DuPont Company in Delaware began experimenting to create a stronger fabric. In the lab they called the result Polymer 6.6, and DuPont claimed that it was almost indestructible. They intended the fabric to be used for women's stockings, and they introduced it at the 1939 New York World's Fair, displayed as a giant stocking on a giant replica of a woman's leg. They named the new fabric nylon after New York, and stores quickly sold out of the new stockings. The first year that nylon stockings were available, women in the United States bought sixty-four million pairs. By 1941 20 percent of all stockings produced in the United States were made of nylon.

The new nylon stockings, or nylons as they came to be called, were very popular with women because they were comfortable, inexpensive, and attractive. In only a few years, however, World War II (1939–45) had started, and nylon was needed for the war. The new fabric was needed to make tents and parachutes and no longer was available for women's accessories. During the war years it was not uncommon for women to draw a black line down the back of their bare legs so that it would appear as if they were wearing stockings. Some women even used makeup to color their legs darker. When nylons appeared in stores again after the war, women lined up by the thousands to buy them and even turned violent in some instances in an effort to get their hands on this commodity that was still in short supply after years of rationing.

By the early 1960s circular knitting machines could create seamless tubes of fabric to make nylon stockings without a back seam, and by the late 1960s very short hemlines had popularized sheer tights called "panty hose," which eliminated the cumbersome garter belt. By the last decades of the twentieth century, most women wore pantyhose or trousers with socks or knee-high stockings. Traditional stockings and garter belts have become rare for day-to-day use, but are still considered elegant and sexy by many, and remain popular lingerie items.

SEE ALSO *Volume 5, 1961–79: Pantyhose*

For More Information

Batterberry, Michael, and Ariane Batterberry. *Fashion: The Mirror of History*. New York: Greenwich House, 1982.

Russell, Bruce. "Synthetic Wonder." *New Straits Times,* January 17, 1988. http://news.google.com/newspapers?nid=1309&dat=19880117&id=P7 BUAAAAIBAJ&sjid=XZADAAAAIBAJ&pg=5411,361405 (accessed on September 4, 2012).

Swim Trunks for Men
• •

Swim trunks, shorts designed to be worn by men while swimming, came into fashion during the mid-1930s. Trunks replaced much bulkier types of swimwear, which covered the entire torso and often had been heavy and hot. Because many men wanted to visit beaches and pools in comfort and wanted ease and freedom of movement in their swimming clothes, they protested the bulky outfits that had been legally required for swimming.

The earliest swimmers probably wore nothing at all in the water. Through the ages, however, various cultures have had different customs of modesty and have imposed restrictions upon swimming and swim-wear accordingly. During the nineteenth century people grew very modest about exposing the body and developed special bathing costumes. Though some English journalists spoke out against the new fashion, stating that wearing clothes while swimming was unsanitary, the extreme modesty of the time won out, and swimmers in Europe and the United States began wearing elaborate swimming costumes. An early men's bathing suit, designed by the Jantzen company in the 1880s, weighed 9 pounds (4 kilograms).

By the early 1900s men's bathing suits had become more stream-lined but still covered much of the body. In 1916 beaches on Chicago's Lake Michigan required men's bathing costumes to be cut no lower on the chest than the armpits. Bathing suit bottoms had to have a "skirt effect" or a long shirt had to be worn over the suit. The bottoms themselves could be no more than 4 inches (10 centimeters) above the knee. A possible alternative was flannel knee pants with a belt and fly front worn with a vest. Failure to obey these rules could result in arrest for indecent exposure.

In the mid-1930s swim trunks came to replace the bulky, restrictive swimwear men were required to wear. © AP IMAGES.

Such modest styles began to change during the 1930s. The invention of a rubberized thread called lycra made a new type of snug-fitting bathing suit possible, and a "nude look" came into fashion on beaches everywhere, with tight, one-piece suits that looked glamorous and made swimming easier. However, men still wanted to swim and relax on beaches bare-chested. In 1933 a men's suit called "the topper" was introduced with a removable tank top that allowed daring men to expose their chests when they wished. That same year the BVD company, which made men's underwear, introduced a line of men's swimwear designed by Olympic swimming champion Johnny Weismuller (1904–1984). The new BVD suit was a tight-fitting one piece with a top made of a series of thin straps that exposed much of the chest, while still remaining within the law.

In the summer of 1936 a male "no shirt movement" led many men to protest the chest-covering requirements. Although topless men were banned from beaches from Atlantic City, New Jersey, to Galveston,

Texas, the men eventually swayed the legislature, and by 1937 it was legal for men to appear in public wearing only swim trunks. Since that time men's swimwear styles have changed little. Into the twenty-first century swim trunks have been either loose-fitting shorts in a "boxer" style or the tighter fitting "brief" style.

SEE ALSO *Volume 3, Nineteenth Century: Bathing Costumes; Volume 4, 1919–29: Swimwear*

For More Information

Lenacek, Lena. *Making Waves: Swimsuits and the Undressing of America*. San Francisco, CA: Chronicle Books, 1989.

Martin, Richard. *Splash!: A History of Swimwear*. New York: Rizzoli, 1990.

Young, William H. and Nancy K. Young. *The 1930s*. Westport, CT: Greenwood, 2002.

Trousers for Women

Throughout much of Western history, women's clothing has been very different from men's clothing, and society has made strict rules requiring individuals to dress according to their gender. In Western cultures for the past several hundred years, these rules have for the most part defined trousers as men's clothing. For centuries, society's disapproval prevented most women from wearing pants. Although in some Eastern cultures, such as those in China or Malaysia, both women and men have long dressed in trousers, most Western cultures have only very recently permitted women to wear them. The trend began during the early 1900s, became more widespread during the 1920s and 1930s, and continued to grow, until by the late 1990s a majority of women regularly wore pants, not only for casual wear but also to work.

It was Eastern culture that inspired French designer Paul Poiret (1879–1944) to become one of the first to design pants for women. In 1913 Poiret created loose-fitting, wide-leg trousers for women called harem pants, which were based on the costumes of the popular opera *Sheherazade*. (Written by Nikola Rimsky-Korsakov [1844–1908] in 1888, *Sheherazade* was based on a famous collection of legends from the Middle East called *1001 Arabian Nights*.)

Trousers have always been the preferred dress of women who had to do physical work. The arrival of World War I (1914–18) gave many

Pants for women continued to be stylish during the 1930s as actresses, such a Marlene Dietrich (pictured) wore trousers regularly. © INTERFOTO/ALAMY.

women jobs, as men went to join the military. Though women who worked with the public still wore skirts, women who worked in factories wore trousers and overalls, not just for comfort but because a skirt might become a workplace hazard. After the war ended women were reluctant to give up the freedom of movement their pants had given them. Another French designer, Gabrielle "Coco" Chanel (1883–1971), loved wearing pants herself, often dressing in her boyfriend's suits, and she began designing pants for women to wear while doing sports and other activities. Chanel designed horseback riding trousers for women, who had previously ridden sidesaddle in heavy skirts.

During the 1930s pants continued to be stylish, although they were still shocking to many. Audiences were both fascinated and horrified by glamorous actresses of the time, such as Marlene Dietrich (c. 1901–1992) and Katharine Hepburn (1909–2003), who wore trousers regularly. Though some designers created tailored slack suits for women, wearing pants was still not widely accepted. Some conservatives considered women in pants unnatural and masculine. However, by 1939 *Vogue,* the respected fashion magazine, pictured women in trousers for the first time, and many women wore pants for playing golf or tennis and riding or bicycling.

During World War II (1939–45) many women were placed in wartime jobs, and trousers once again got a boost in popularity. Although the very feminine look of the postwar 1950s discouraged many women from wearing pants, by the 1960s and 1970s extremely casual clothes were the fashion, and with blue jeans becoming the *de facto* uniform of Western youth of both genders, it wasn't long before pants on women became completely accepted, first for casual wear and finally for the workplace. Fashion leaders such as Yves Saint Laurent (1936–) designed dressy pantsuits. By the late 1990s two-thirds of women in the United States wore pants to work several times a week.

For More Information

Berry, Sarah. *Screen Style: Fashion and Femininity in 1930s Hollywood.* Minneapolis, MN: University of Minnesota Press, 2000.

Ewing, Elizabeth. *History of Twentieth Century Fashion.* Revised by Alice Mackrell. Lanham, MD: Barnes and Noble, 1989.

T-Shirt

Originally designed to be hidden under other clothes, the T-shirt has become one of the essential elements of casual fashion in the United States and around the world. The T-shirt, so-called because of its letter T-like shape, was issued as an undergarment to servicemen during both World War I (1914–18) and World War II (1939–45). Made of soft cotton fabric, the short-sleeved T-shirt was much more comfortable than the woolen undergarments that had been typical since 1880, and it quickly became a favorite with soldiers and sailors alike.

The hard work of war soon found military men stripping down to their white T-shirts to do their jobs in relative comfort. By the end of World War II in 1945, pictures of sailors and soldiers working in nothing more than pants and T-shirts had become quite common. In 1942 T-shirted military men even appeared on the cover of *Life* magazine, one of the most popular magazines of the time, marking the transition of the T-shirt from undershirt to an acceptable outer shirt.

Servicemen's return home soon made the T-shirt an essential part of working men's wardrobes. The popularity of the T-shirt was further fueled by Hollywood. Films featuring male film stars in T-shirts associated the shirts with masculine power, sexuality, and youthful rebellion. Handsome Marlon Brando (1924–2004) wore a T-shirt that showed off his muscular build in the 1951 feature film *A Streetcar Named Desire,* and James Dean's (1931–1955) role in *Rebel without a Cause* (1955) linked the T-shirt with youthful distrust of authority figures.

Soon T-shirts were used to make political statements or simply to express a point of view. During the Vietnam War (1954–75) plain white T-shirts worn by young men associated them with a conservative political attitude, while more liberal (progressive) men wore tie-dyed or

T-shirts, once worn only by servicemen under their clothes, soon displayed names of universities and sports teams. © BETTMANN/HISTORICAL/CORBIS.

painted T-shirts. Women began to use the T-shirt to make their own statements during the sexual revolution of the 1960s and 1970s. The T-shirt's clingy fabric accentuated women's shapeliness.

The symbolism of T-shirts became much more obvious when T-shirts started carrying written messages. T-shirts displayed the widest range of opinions and messages, from the pleasant "Have a Nice Day" to offensive profanity, and from college university names to professional sports teams. T-shirts turned their wearers into walking billboards for popular brands such as Nike or Old Navy. Whether you wanted to show your love of a local college, a brand of soda pop, or a favorite rock band, there was a T-shirt for you. At the beginning of the twenty-first century T-shirts continued to be an essential component of wardrobes around the world and were, along with blue jeans and sneakers, the foremost examples of American fashion.

For More Information
Harris, Alice. *The White T.* New York: HarperCollins, 1996.

Young, William H. and Nancy K. Young. *World War II and the Postwar Years in America: A Historical and Cultural Encyclopedia.* Santa Barbara, California: ABC-CLIO, 2010.

Women's Dresses

Women's dresses had gone to great extremes in the 1920s, with very short hemlines and boyish styles. The change in dress styles in the 1930s was thus very dramatic, for the decade saw a return to femininity and distinct changes in cut and hemline. The depressed economic circumstances of the decade and later of the war years required simplicity in dress styles, but talented designers turned these constraints to their advantage, making slim-fitting but stylish dresses in a variety of styles.

Printed fabrics allowed even plainly tailored women's dresses to show decoration.
© BETTMANN/HISTORICAL/ CORBIS.

Perhaps the single biggest change in the 1930s was the lengthening of the hemline, which fell to mid-calf for day wear and to the floor for evening wear. Dresses were tube-shaped and very sleek, fitting closely through the torso and lacking billows or pleats in the skirt. Dressmakers achieved a flowing look either by using newer fabrics like rayon or by cutting fabrics diagonal to the direction of the weave, called a bias cut. Waists in general were tucked in closely, and the waistline was often accented with a belt. Late in the 1930s the desire for a very small waist led to the reappearance of the corset, a confining undergarment that had gone out of style in the 1910s. Wartime dress restrictions soon put an end to this fashion revival, however, much to the pleasure of women who did not want to see the return of the uncomfortable corset.

Several elements of 1930s and early 1940s dress styles are especially distinctive. The first was the treatment of the back and buttocks. Many dresses were made to reveal large portions of the back, with great Vs that reached nearly to the waist, meaning the top neckline of the dress plunged down to the waist in the back creating a V shape. Dresses also were fitted very closely across the buttocks, marking the first time in history the true shape of women's rears were made a focus of attention. These styles were particularly visible in evening wear.

Another significant trend during the 1930s was the emergence of the print dress. Women bought simple dresses without fancy tailoring or decorative touches to save money, but they didn't want to look plain. Many women turned to printed fabrics as the solution. Checks, polka dots, flowers, and a variety of free-flowing designs in fabric allowed women to make a plain dress pretty.

The coming of World War II in 1939 brought further economizing to women's dresses. Hemlines rose once more to the knee or slightly above the knee, and fabrics such as rayon and silk that were needed for military use were rarely used. The basic dress styles did not change until 1947, when the New Look styles brought a new revolution in women's dress.

SEE ALSO *Volume 4, 1919–29: Hemlines; Volume 5, 1946–60: New Look*

For More Information

Baker, Patricia. *Fashions of a Decade: The 1940s*. New York: Facts on File, 1992.

Behnke, Alison Marie. *The Little Black Dress and Zoot Suits: Depression and Wartime Fashions From the 1930s*. Minneapolis, MN: Twenty-First Century Books, 2012.

Costantino, Maria. *Fashions of a Decade: The 1930s.* New York: Facts on File, 1992.

Laver, James. *Costume and Fashion: A Concise History.* 4th ed. London, England: Thames and Hudson, 2002.

Payne, Blanche, Geitel Winakor, and Jane Farrell-Beck. *The History of Costume.* 2nd ed. New York: HarperCollins, 1992.

Women's Suits

One of the most common outfits worn by women of the 1930s and early 1940s was the suit, a basic ensemble that paired a matching skirt and jacket with a blouse. Women's suits were one of the few choices of business wear for women, along with the skirt and shirtwaist or blouse, but they also were commonly worn for any type of daytime activity. All variety of fabrics could be used for women's suits, from wool tweed for cooler weather to silk or rayon, also known as artificial silk, for dressier occasions.

Following the general trends in women's dress during this period, the skirts with women's suits were very simple, without pleats or elaborate tailoring. They hung straight from the waist to a varying length from just below the knee to mid-calf. The matching jacket, however, was a much more versatile garment. In general jackets fit the body closely, and most had a cinched waist. The small waist was defined by a decorative belt or by tailoring that drew the jacket in sharply at the waist. Suits that flared at the hips accented the waistline. Another prominent feature of women's suits in the 1930s was wide shoulders. Shoulders were made to look broad and square with tailoring or padding. Necklines, most often cut in a deep V shape, where the neckline plunged to the waist creating a V shape, to show off the blouse or neck ruff, could have lapels, or flaps on the front of a coat that fold back against the chest, similar to a man's suit.

One of the fashion innovations of the 1930s was women's use of the pants suit, also known as the slacks suit. Like many of the popular fashions of the 1930s, the pants suit was associated with a Hollywood starlet. Actress Marlene Dietrich (c. 1901–1992) wore men's clothes in many of her movies, but she was especially known for wearing masculine suits in her public appearances. Women's pants suits generally had flared or bell-bottomed trousers, and the jackets were tailored in slightly softer versions of men's styles. Pantsuits were considered a little outrageous during the 1930s and 1940s, because people were still adjusting to the idea of women wearing pants.

SEE ALSO *Volume 4, 1930–45: Men's Suits*

For More Information

Bigelow, Marybelle S. *Fashion in History: Apparel in the Western World.* Minneapolis, MN: Burgess Publishing, 1970.

Costantino, Maria. *Fashions of a Decade: The 1930s.* New York: Facts on File, 1992.

Hatt, Christine. *Clothes of the Early Modern World.* Columbus, OH: Peter Bedrick Books, 2002.

Payne, Blanche, Geitel Winakor, and Jane Farrell-Beck. *The History of Costume.* 2nd ed. New York: HarperCollins, 1992.

Zoot Suit

The zoot suit was an exaggerated version of a typical double-breasted (two rows of buttons down the front) business suit of the 1940s, altered to make it both more casual and more hip. Very popular among young African American men, young Mexican American men, and others trying to look hip and current, the zoot suit had a long jacket with wide shoulder pads and narrow hips, and high-waisted baggy trousers with tightly pegged, or narrowed, cuffs. Zoot suits were often made in bright colors and worn with long watch chains, brightly patterned neckties, flat topped "pork pie" hats, and shoes with thick soles. The zoot suit style was closely identified with jazz music and the casual youth lifestyle of the 1940s.

Many different people have claimed to be the inventor of the zoot suit. In reality the style probably had its roots among poor black youth of the Great Depression era (1929–39). Unable to afford new clothes, many young African Americans wore suits belonging to older relatives, taking them in at the waist, hips, and ankles. A tailor and bandleader in Chicago, Illinois, named Harold C. Fox (1910–1996) claimed to have made the first zoot suit in 1941 because he liked the style of the cut-down suits he saw on poor urban teenagers. Fox and others liked the style because it was snug enough to look cool, yet loose enough to do the latest jazz dances. The new suit style became part of African American jazz culture from New York's Harlem neighborhood to New Orleans,

Louisiana's French Quarter. It was common jazz slang to put a "z" at the beginning of words, so the suit became a zoot.

The new zoot suit soon spread to the West Coast, where young Mexican American men took up the fashion. The pride and sense of identity that the zoot suit culture inspired in youth of color was threatening to many conservative whites, and some even reacted violently to the sight of young men wearing the distinctive zoot suit. Perhaps the most extreme examples of this violence were the "zoot suit riots" that occurred in Los Angeles, California, in June 1943 and spread to other cities such as Chicago, New York, Philadelphia, and Detroit. Beginning after a fight between a few sailors and a few young people in zoot suits, the riots spread and lasted for two weeks, with hundreds of uniformed white sailors and servicemen attacking young Mexican and African Americans, beating them and ripping off their suits. The police did little to stop the violence, and local newspapers spoke out in support of the servicemen's actions.

Once World War II (1939–45) began, fabric rationing caused the U.S. government to ban the manufacture of the zoot suit, and those wearing banned styles were often ostracized and labeled by others as unpatriotic. The style never became widespread again, though the extremely baggy fashions popular among the youth of the 1990s and 2000s can be seen as a descendant of the zoot suit.

The flamboyant styling of the zoot suit captured the exuberance of the jazz culture with which it was associated.
© FOTOMATON/ALAMY.

SEE ALSO *Volume 4, 1930–45: Men's Suits; Volume 5, 1980–99: Baggy Jeans*

For More Information

Behnke, Alison Marie. *The Little Black Dress and Zoot Suits: Depression and Wartime Fashions From the 1930s.* Minneapolic, MN: Twenty-First Century Books, 2012.

Thorne, Tony. *Fads, Fashions, and Cults: From Acid House to Zoot Suit.* London, England: Trafalgar Square, 1994.

Tyler, Bruce. "Zoot-Suit Culture and the Black Press." *Journal of American Culture* (Summer 1994): 21–35.

White, Shane, and Graham J. White. *Stylin': African American Expressive Culture, from Its Beginnings to the Zoot Suit.* Ithaca, NY: Cornell University Press, 1999.

Headwear, 1930–45

The severe hairstyles of the 1920s were replaced with softer styles between 1930 and 1945. Men and women grew their hair out slightly from the short styles popular in the previous decade. Men abandoned their slick, flattened styles in favor of clean, loose hair. Women, for the most part, wore their hair cut neatly above their shoulders, but some experimented briefly with longer styles inspired by glamorous movie stars such as Veronica Lake (1919–1973).

The most characteristic look of this period was waved hair. Both men and women encouraged any natural wave their hair might have or visited hairdressers for permanent or temporary waved styles. Men might not admit to professional help, however, as fashion trends favored natural waves for men. Women could freely wave their hair in many different ways: naturally, with the help of a variety of curlers, or with a professionally styled permanent.

Most men were clean-shaven, except for older men who could not bring themselves to part with their beards. Negative attitudes about beards during this time were vividly described in the *New Statesman and Nation* in August 1935 and quoted by Richard Corson in *Fashions in Hair: The First Five Thousand Years*: "a bearded man in America enjoys all the privileges of a bearded woman in a circus." The sentiment seemed to be true throughout the Western world. Although men shaved regularly, many kept neat mustaches, which they waxed, ironed, or trimmed daily. Eager for any way to make shaving even easier, men quickly embraced the electric shaver introduced in 1935, which allowed them to shave without water.

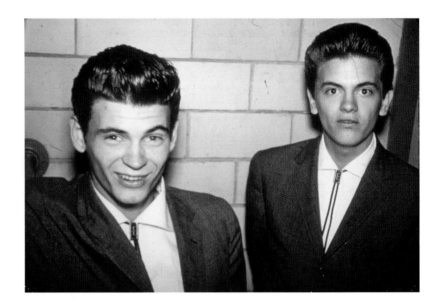

Both men and women wore hats during this period. Men continued to wear fedoras, a soft, crowned felt hat, but in many more colors than before. Felt hats came in a wide variety of colors: brown, dark or light gray, grayish blue, green, and even lilac. The most unusual colors were popularized by the flashy outfits worn by gangsters, who were prominent in the news of the time. Women's hats remained small but not as close-fitting as the cloche hat of the 1920s. Women wore small brimmed hats or flat berets perched at an angle on top of their heads.

For More Information

Corson, Richard. *Fashions in Hair: The First Five Thousand Years*. London, England: Peter Owen, 2001.

Lister, Margot. *Costume: An Illustrated Survey from Ancient Times to the Twentieth Century*. London, England: Herbert Jenkins, 1967.

Trasko, Mary. *Daring Do's: A History of Extraordinary Hair*. New York: Flammarion, 1994.

Electric Shaver

With the advent of the electronic age, inventors and visionaries wanted to employ electric current to simplify and improve everyday living. Out of this desire came the electric, or dry, shaver, a device that employs electrically powered blades, rather than old-fashioned soap, water, and razor blades, to remove body hair.

Before the electric shaver was successfully marketed, quite a few attempts were made to develop and promote variations of the device. The initial electric shaver patent was issued in 1898. A typical early model was called Lektro-shav and was sold in the 1910s. In order to work, a Lek-tro-shav had to be connected to a lightbulb socket. In the mid-1920s came the Vibro-Shave, whose handle included a tiny magnet and spring that also depended upon a lightbulb socket for its electric current.

Jacob Schick (1878–1937), a career U.S. Army officer, is credited as the inventor of what evolved into the modern-era electric shaver. Schick initially devised a shaver powered by an external motor but could find no one to market it. Returning to the development of conventional, non-electric methods, he invented what he called the Magazine Repeating Razor in 1921. This was a predecessor of the injector razor, in which replacement blades were kept in the razor handle and were fed into position without having to touch the blade. Schick formed his own company and began selling this razor in 1926. Despite his early success, he continued to invent. He was determined to develop a dry shaver and did so in 1927. Schick's first electric shaver included a tiny motor and shaving head that were connected via a bendable shaft. The head consisted of cutters that reciprocated, or went back and forth in a repeating motion. By the end of the decade Schick established a second company, Schick Dry Shaver, Inc., to produce and market his invention. Sales initially were slow, but upgraded models were developed and the product gradually caught on with the public. The Schick Model S, the first to replace Jacob Schick's prototype was marketed in 1935. Two years later 1.5 million Schick electric shavers were sold. Meanwhile, other companies began producing electric shavers. Among the types marketed during the 1930s were the Remington Model E, Sunbeam Shavemaster, Arvin Consort, Braun Standard 50, and Rolls Razor Viceroy.

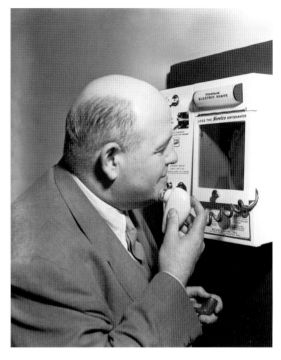

Because being clean shaven remained in style, men embraced the convenience of electric shavers. © BETTMANN/ HISTORICAL/CORBIS.

An engineer named Alexandre Horowitz (1904–1982) invented the rotary electric shaver, which employed rotating cutters. Horowitz was employed by the Netherlands-based N.V. Philips Gloeilampenfabrieken (Royal Philips Electronics), a producer of radios and lightbulbs. Working with Schick's shaver, Horowitz developed his own rotating razor. Philips first marketed the rotary shaver in 1939; it was called the Philishave shaver. Horowitz's invention featured a single head; two-headed models were devised during World War II (1939–45) and marketed after the war. The various models of electric shavers were all welcomed by men seeking convenience and interested in the possibilities of electricity.

For More Information

Corson, Richard. *Fashions in Hair: The First Five Thousand Years*. London, England: Peter Owen, 2001.

Krumholz, Phillip L. *A History of Shaving and Razors*. Bartonville, IL: Ad Libs Publishing, 1987.

Peek-a-Boo Bang

When film actress Veronica Lake (1919–1973) appeared in the movie *I Wanted Wings* in 1941 she started a craze for a new hairstyle, the peek-a-boo bang. Her long blonde hair was parted on the left side, softly curled under at the ends, and often slipped in front of her face to cover her right eye. Her on-screen beauty quickly made her a box office star and inspired many American women to copy her hairstyle.

The peek-a-boo bang was a sexy style but very impractical, even for Lake herself. According to Richard Corson in *Fashions in Hair: The First Five Thousand Years, LIFE* magazine informed readers that "her hair catches fire fairly often when she is smoking." Working women found the style a real nuisance because it constantly blocked their vision as they bent over their work. For factory workers the style was actually dangerous; their dangling hair would often get tangled in machinery and cause work stoppages. But it took the government to end the craze for this impractical hairstyle. The fad became so disruptive to work in war plants in 1942 that U.S. government officials asked Lake to stop wearing her hair long for the duration of World War II (1939–45). Women switched to wearing more practical shorter styles or swept back pompadours.

For More Information

Corson, Richard. *Fashions in Hair: The First Five Thousand Years.* London, England: Peter Owen, 2001.

Lenburg, Jeff. *Peekaboo: the Story of Veronica Lake.* Lincoln, NE: St. Martin's Press, 2001.

Trasko, Mary. *Daring Do's: A History of Extraordinary Hair.* New York: Flammarion, 1994.

Pompadour

The pompadour, an elaborate hairstyle where long hair is swept up into a tall arrangement of curls or smooth waves on the top of the head, has been popular at many different times in history, mostly among women, though some men have worn pompadours as well. During the early 1940s many fashionable women wore their hair in a pompadour style, brushing their hair up into a roll worn high on the forehead. Sometimes, the pompadour was just worn at the front of the hair, with the back left in long curls, and sometimes all of the hair was pulled up behind the front pompadour roll.

The pompadour took its name from an eighteenth-century Frenchwoman, Jean Antoinette Poisson (1721–1764), the Marquise de Pompadour. The marquise, as a woman of noble ranking in Europe was often referred, was the mistress of Louis XV (1710–1774), king of France. She was famous for her vast and expensive wardrobe and was the model for much of French fashion at the time. Her hairstyle, brushed straight back and lifted high above her forehead, was given the name "pompadour" after her. In the court of Louis XV and throughout the centuries that followed, many women have imitated the Marquise de Pompadour's elegant hairstyle.

The early 1940s still felt the pinch of the economic depression that had marked the 1930s. One result of the almost universal financial hardship was that many people looked to the movies for escape and entertainment. Copying the glamorous hairstyles of film stars became a way to rise above the grim reality of day-to-day life, and an elaborate hairdo did not cost much more than a simple one. During World War II (1939–45) many fabrics and other sewing supplies were rationed because the government needed them for the war, and civilians could only obtain limited quantities. As during the Great Depression (1929–39), women could still express their sense of individuality and fashion cheaply by changing their hairstyles. Many popular hairstyles of the day involved elaborate arrangements of curls and waves. Film stars such as Joan Crawford (1908–1973) and popular singers like the Andrews Sisters charmed audiences with their hair swept up in a pompadour, and many women of the 1940s imitated their look.

During the late 1940s a more masculine and military look took over women's fashions, and the glamorous hairstyles were abandoned. The pompadour would return in a surprising way on the heads of rebellious young men of the 1950s and early 1960s. One of the most famous male pompadours was worn by rock idol Elvis Presley (1935–1977).

For More Information

Sherrow, Victoria. *Encyclopedia of Hair: A Cultural History*. Westport, CT: Greenwood Press, 2006.

Turudich, Daniela. *1940s Hairstyles*. Long Beach, CA: Streamline Press, 2002.

Waved Hair

Women adopted more feminine hairstyles between 1930 and 1945, growing out the boyish, short styles that had been popular in the previous decade. Though their hair was longer during this period, especially throughout the 1930s, women still wore what would be considered short hair; their styles were just softer and less severe than they had been during the 1920s. To soften their look, women waved their hair. They created waves at home by wrapping their damp hair around cloth strips, their fingers, or by securing their damp curls with bobby pins until they dried. Fake curls could be pinned to the head and were especially popular to wear with hats to accent the temples or in back of the head to make the hair look longer. At salons women could permanently wave their hair or get a wave made with a heated iron and held in place with Macassar oil, a hair conditioner that had been popular since the Victorian era (1837–1901). This product, made from a mixture of ylang-ylang oil and coconut oil, was named after the district of Macassar in eastern Indonesia where these exotic ingredients were purchased. Hair held in place with Macassar oil would usually stay in place nearly a week.

Men also wore wavy hair at this time. While women created unnatural waves and curls all over their head, men's waves were made to look more natural. Any natural wave in a man's hair was often created by running the fingers through the hair. This created more body, or wave, in the hair instead of being plastered down as it had been in the previous decade. If a man had naturally straight hair he might go to a hairdresser or barber for help, but he would probably not admit to this if asked, because it was not considered appropriate for men to get permanent waves at this time. However, straight hair was almost never seen on either men or women during this period.

For More Information

Cheang, Sarah and Geraldine Biddle-Perry eds. *Hair: Styling, Culture and Fashion.* New York: Berg Publishers, 2008.

Corson, Richard. *Fashions in Hair: The First Five Thousand Years.* London, England: Peter Owen, 2001.

Trasko, Mary. *Daring Do's: A History of Extraordinary Hair.* New York: Flammarion, 1994.

Body Decorations, 1930–45

The extravagant, frivolous fashions of the 1920s were replaced by more practical decorations and accessories during the 1930s. The Great Depression (1929–39) and World War II (1939–45) put pressure on both men and women to simplify their wardrobes. The fanciful purses of the 1920s were replaced by the plainer clutch purse style, for example. Rather than buying different jewelry to adorn each different outfit, women instead favored simple styles or wore meaningful pieces to which they could add decoration, such as charm bracelets.

One trend for excess continued during these lean years, however. The fashion for wearing heavy makeup started during the 1920s lasted well into the next decades. Women "blushed" their cheeks with rouge, darkened their lips with a variety of lipsticks, and lengthened and thickened their eyelashes with mascara. According to Jane Mulvagh in *Vogue History of 20th Century Fashion*, in 1931 *Vogue* magazine reported that "we are all painted ladies today," adding: "Now we feel undressed unless we have the right shade of face powder, and if we lose our lipstick, we lose our strongest moral support." The rationing, or limiting, of luxuries during World War II highlighted the importance of makeup. Mulvagh noted that the British government "tried to ban cosmetics at the outbreak of war, but fortunately withdrew this ruling." Lipstick and rouge, she pointed out, were "the last unrationed, if scarce, indulgences of feminine expression during austerity [severe economy], and were vital for morale."

Men simplified their looks more than women did. With the rising popularity of sporty clothing styles during the 1930s and beyond, men abandoned other forms of ornament such as canes and pocket watches. The only pieces of jewelry men typically wore were a wedding ring if they were married, pins to hold down the collars of their button-up shirts when they wore a tie and, if they were in the military, a metal identification bracelet.

For More Information

Costantino, Maria. *Fashions of a Decade: The 1930s.* New York: Chelsea House, 2007.

Lister, Margot. *Costume: An Illustrated Survey from Ancient Times to the Twentieth Century.* London, England: Herbert Jenkins, 1967.

Mulvagh, Jane. *Vogue History of 20th Century Fashion.* New York: Viking, 1988.

Payne, Blanche, Geitel Winakor, and Jane Farrell-Beck. *The History of Costume.* 2nd ed. New York: HarperCollins, 1992.

Charm Bracelet

A charm bracelet is a chain of silver or gold, worn around the wrist, to which individual jewelry symbols, called charms, are attached. Traditionally, the wearer, usually a woman, begins with a simple chain then chooses and adds charms that have personal meaning to her own life. Though jewelry bearing charms has been worn through the ages, the modern wave of popularity of the charm bracelet began in the United States during the 1940s and lasted into the early 1960s.

Originally a charm was an object that was thought to provide luck or protection to one who wore or carried it. Good luck charms, also called amulets, were worn on jewelry on the wrist and around the neck at least as far back as ancient Egypt, in about 3000 B.C.E. Around 500 B.C.E. the Assyrians, Babylonians, and Persians wore bracelets to which they attached small objects they believed had special powers. The modern charm bracelet fad began in England during the late 1800s, when Queen Victoria (1819–1901) began wearing a gold chain with lockets that contained portraits of her family. This introduced a new identity for the charm bracelet, as decorative jewelry with a personal meaning, rather than an amulet for protection or luck, and many women copied the queen by hanging glass beads and lockets from their bracelets.

During the 1940s, as American soldiers traveled through the cities of Europe and Asia, they picked up small jewelry charms as souvenirs to take back as gifts to the women in their lives. Women attached these to bracelets that soon became quite popular, and American jewelers began to produce small symbols specifically for charm bracelets. By the 1950s charm bracelets had become a part of American middle-class girlhood. Often the chain, in gold or silver, was given to a girl before she reached her teens, and charms were added throughout her life. Usually the charms symbolized turning points in the wearer's life, such as a sixteenth birthday, graduation, wedding, or the birth of children. Some charms represented interests or hobbies. A girl who loved horses might hang a silver horse or saddle from her bracelet; one who played tennis might buy or be given a golden tennis racquet. Charm bracelets thus became prized personal heirlooms, passed down to daughters and granddaughters.

Charm bracelets faded from popularity during the very casual fashions of the late 1960s and early 1970s, but they had a revival during the 1980s. Then, however, young women did not put together their personal bracelets but rather bought older charm bracelets that had been put together during the 1950s as part of a vintage, or antique, look. By the early twenty-first century fashion designers such as Louis Vuitton were introducing new charm bracelets. As with the revived fashion of the 1950s, the charms on these new bracelets often, but not always, had no particular personal significance to the wearer. One notable exception were Pandora bracelets, created almost twenty years earlier in Denmark and successfully introduced in North America in 2003. Designed with special threads that allow for easy interchangeability, Pandora beads were available in many varieties that celebrated milestones in a person's life, such as graduation, marriage, or the birth of a child.

For More Information

Bracken, Thomas. *Good Luck Symbols and Talismans*. Philadelphia, PA: Chelsea House Publishers, 1998.

Ettinger, Roseann. *Popular Jewelry, 1840–1940*. 2nd ed. Atglen, PA: Schiffer Publishing, 1997.

Payne, Blanche, Geitel Winakor, and Jane Farrell-Beck. *The History of Costume*. 2nd ed. New York: HarperCollins, 1992.

Schwartz, Joanne, Robert N. Schwartz, and Joan (CON) Munkacsi. *Charms and Charm Bracelets: The Complete Guide*. Atglen, PA: Schiffer Pub Limited, 2005.

Most clutch purses have a metal hinged clasp or snap closure. © KELLIS/ SHUTTERSTOCK.COM.

Clutch Purse

As more women entered the workforce, the decorative beaded handbags and more fanciful embroidered or tapestry purses of previous years were limited to dressy evening events. The clutch purse became the standard for business or daytime activities. The clutch purse was a small leather or smooth, stiffened cloth purse with a metal hinged clasp or snap closure. Clutch purses were often neat, flat rectangles made of a plain color. Leather clutches were most often black or brown, but cloth purses could be of a color that complemented a woman's dress. Flat, tailored clutch purses were later replaced with larger purses, known as satchel purses, which women stuffed with necessities and slung over their shoulders. Satchel purses became especially popular during World War II (1939–45), when women needed to carry more things as they walked or rode public transportation to conserve gas for the war effort. Clutch purses are still often seen as practical items, and have remained very popular well into the twenty-first century, with many retailers and fashion designers offering a myriad of different colors and styles.

For More Information

Bigelow, Marybelle S. *Fashion in History: Apparel in the Western World.* Minneapolis, MN: Burgess Publishing, 1970.

Johnson, Anna. *Handbags: The Power of the Purse.* New York: Workman Publishing, 2002.

Payne, Blanche, Geitel Winakor, and Jane Farrell-Beck. *The History of Costume.* 2nd ed. New York: HarperCollins, 1992.

Mascara

Named after the Spanish word for "mask," mascara is a type of makeup that is applied to the eyelashes to make them appear darker, longer, and thicker. Though women, and occasionally men, have applied darkeners to their eyelashes for centuries, modern mascara was first created and sold around 1915, the beginning of a time when cosmetics were becoming increasingly popular.

At many different times women have used substances to alter their appearance according to the fashion of the day, so the idea of mascara is not new. For example, around 400 B.C.E. ancient Greek women rubbed powdery black incense into their eyelashes for a dramatic appearance. In the post–Civil War (1861–65) United States, wealthy northern women shocked older society by wearing mascara on their eyes as a sign of prosperity. Mascara first became socially acceptable during the early 1900s, as women began to express their independence and seek an energetic, sexy new fashion. Along with the traditional dark mascara, made fashionable by popular film stars of the time, there also was brightly colored mascara with applicators that looked like crayons.

In 1915 an American named T. L. Williams noticed that his sister Mabel colored her lashes with a petroleum jelly called Vaseline, mixed with coal dust for color. He began to package and sell the product, calling it Maybelline. Williams sold his mascara successfully through the mail until the 1930s. Then, the heavy use of cosmetics had become so fashionable that more and more women wanted to buy mascara. In 1932 Maybelline created a special package of mascara that sold in stores for ten cents.

Early mascara was packaged in cakes with a tiny brush for applying it. A woman would wet the brush and then rub it on the cake of mascara to create a paste to carefully brush over the lashes. In 1957 famous

Though women have used powders to darken their eyelashes for thousands of years, mascara has been sold in stores only since 1932. © VALUA VITALY/ SHUTTERSTOCK.COM.

cosmetics manufacturer Helena Rubenstein (1870–1965) invented a liquid form of mascara that came in a tube with a brush inside.

For women who use cosmetics, and for some men, such as rock musicians, who wish to create a dramatic impression, mascara has remained popular into the twenty-first century. Though the general use of mascara to thicken and darken eyelashes has remained the same, there have been various improvements, such as the creation of waterproof mascara, non-irritating mascara, and mascara that curls the lashes.

For More Information

Maybelline. http://www.maybelline.com (accessed on September 4, 2012).

Peiss, Kathy Lee. *Hope in a Jar: The Making of America's Beauty Culture.* New York: Metropolitan Books, 1998.

Footwear, 1930–45

The types of shoes worn by men and women during the 1930s were greatly determined by the effects of the Great Depression (1929–39) on their lives. Those impoverished by the Depression wore old styles, sometimes with holes in the soles. Others, who were lucky enough to gain wealth during this difficult time, set new trends in leisure wear that would influence the clothing of the masses following World War II (1939–45). Rationing, or limiting, of materials needed for shoes, such as leather and rubber, during the war introduced new practical styles of footwear.

The most fashionable men wore a variety of shoes before the war. White Bucs, or buckskin shoes with rubber soles, were popular with Europeans, and especially Americans, whose love of sport and leisure wear continued to grow. Bucs complemented the comfortable knit shirts and loose pants worn on vacation and while watching or playing sports. More formal leather shoes, including wing tips, were worn for business. During and after the war, men began to favor heavier soled shoes made from thick leather. Military boots called bluchers, which looked like heavy, blunt-toed oxfords, became especially popular among servicemen and college students. These thicker styles were part of the Bold Look for men that came into fashion later in the 1940s.

The Depression and the war interrupted a trend in women's footwear toward more glamour and women favored more practical styles of laced oxfords. The 1930s saw the introduction of a new feminine style called the peep-toed shoe that offered a glimpse of a woman's toes peeking out

The footwear of the 1930s and World War II offered practicality as well as style.
© LAKE COUNTY MUSEUM/ CORBIS MUSEUM/CORBIS.

from a cutout at the tip of the shoe's toe. By the mid-1930s designers experimented with platform sandals featuring tall wood or cork soles and padded leather straps. One of the most distinctive styles featured gold-colored leather straps with a cork sole of six different colored layers. As the war drew closer, women abandoned these glamorous styles for more practical shoes. Lower-heeled pumps and oxfords became the most popular. Cloth and felt uppers replaced leather as supplies of the sturdy hide were restricted to the war effort. After the war women quickly returned to wearing the beautiful shoe styles of prewar times.

For More Information

Lawlor, Laurie. *Where Will This Shoe Take You?: A Walk Through the History of Footwear.* New York: Walker and Co., 1996.

Lister, Margot. *Costume: An Illustrated Survey from Ancient Times to the Twentieth Century.* London, England: Herbert Jenkins, 1967.

Mulvagh, Jane. *Vogue History of 20th Century Fashion.* New York: Viking, 1988.

Pratt, Lucy, and Linda Woolley. *Shoes.* London, England: V&A Publications, 1999.

Young, William H. *Shoes.* Westport, CT: Greenwood Press, 2002.

Military Boots

Soldiers in combat often find themselves trudging through dense forests or arid deserts, or climbing up mountains in weather conditions ranging from steamy hot to icy cold. In such situations the type of military boot they have been issued will play a key role in their individual survival, not to mention their effectiveness in battle. While this seems logical, it was not fully acknowledged by the American military until World War II (1939–45), when it was recognized that standard-issue leather boots were not suitable for all soldiers in all combat situations.

For centuries soldiers have worn military boots. Often such footwear covered half the leg, running all the way up to the knee, permitting the wearer to tuck in his trousers. A solidly built military boot was preferable to a common shoe, yet the importance of proper footwear for all soldiers went unacknowledged. For example, during the War of 1812 (1812–15), boots were issued only to generals and general staff officers, and not to common foot soldiers. In the American Civil War (1861–65), Union army artillerymen and cavalrymen (those fighting for the North) were issued boots while infantrymen, the soldiers most likely to spend long amounts of time marching, were issued only shoes.

Eventually, military boots became more than just status symbols that were worn by officers but denied to infantrymen. Military boots soon were worn by all military men, regardless of rank. While military boot styles evolved across the decades, they always were standardized. Some were knee-length, while others only reached the ankle; they were laced, made of leather, and either black or dark brown.

Different types of boots for different types of terrain and tasks help keep military and civilian feet safe from the elements. © ANDREY STEPANOV/SHUTTERSTOCK. COM.

The realization that inadequate clothing directly resulted in increased casualties evolved from experiences in World War II battles. During the campaign to take the Aleutian Islands, located 1,200 miles (1,931 kilometers) from the Alaskan Peninsula, from the Japanese, the majority of noncombat casualties resulted from inadequate clothing and overexposure to the cold climate. Trench foot, which resembles frostbite and is a direct result of prolonged exposure to moisture and the elements, also became a common problem among soldiers. In the final phases of the campaign, American soldiers were supplied with more appropriate cold-weather clothing, which included the substitution of insulated arctic shoes for leather boots.

In the decades after World War II, different types of military boots were designed for different terrain as wars have brought American soldiers into the jungles of Vietnam and the deserts of the Middle East. In 1965 fast-drying nonleather boots with nylon uppers were issued to soldiers heading off to Vietnam. Latter-day military boots feature ripple soles: soles that look like teeth and allow the boot to more firmly grip the terrain. They also include removable inner soles.

The attention the military gave to boot styles brought this footwear to the attention of the public around World War II. Military boots called bluchers became especially popular with young civilian, or nonmilitary, men in the 1940s. Bluchers were heavy-soled, black leather, laced shoes; they looked like thick-soled, clunky oxfords. Bluchers were worn on college campuses across the United States and Europe. By the twenty-first century all types of military boots and shoes were sold on the commercial marketplace and remained favorite styles for young people.

For More Information

Cureton, Charles. *The U.S. Marine Corps: The Illustrated History of the American Soldier, His Uniform and His Equipment.* London, England: Greenhill Books, 1997.

Quartermaster General of the Army. *U.S. Army Uniforms and Equipment, 1889.* Lincoln, NE: University of Nebraska Press, 1986.

Stanton, Shelby. *U.S. Army Uniforms of World War II.* Mechanicsburg, PA: Stackpole Books, 1991.

Troiani, Don, Earl J. Coates, and Michael J. McAfee. *Don Troiani's Regiments and Uniforms of the Civil War.* Mechanicsburg, PA: Stackpole Books, 2002.

Peep-Toed Shoes

One of the more popular women's shoe styles of the 1930s was the peep-toed shoe, so named for the provocative view that it offered of the tips of the toes. Peep-toed shoes came in a variety of styles, but they typically had a high heel, a small upper that covered the sides of the foot and the instep, a strap around the heel and, of course, a small hole in the upper, right at the point of the shoe that revealed the toes. Once open-toed shoes were only proper to wear on vacations at resorts, but now peep-toes shoes became acceptable for many daytime leisure activities. According to Lucy Pratt and Linda Woolley in their book *Shoes,* during World War II (1939–45) peep-toed shoes were banned as "frivolous and potentially 'dangerous.'" But when the war ended, women craving the glamour and feminine styling of high-heeled, peep-toed shoes brought the style back into favor. In subsequent years, the hole at the tip of the shoe grew larger, allowing more of the foot to be seen. Adding to the allure, painting the toenails with nail polish would add a colorful contrast to the look, allowing women to express their individual sense of style without a great deal of additional expense.

SEE ALSO *Volume 5, 1946–60: Plastic Shoe*

For More Information

Mendes, Valerie and Amy De La Haye. *Fashion since 1900.* 2nd Ed. London, England: Thames and Hudson, 2010.
Mulvagh, Jane. *Vogue History of 20th Century Fashion.* New York: Viking, 1988.
Pratt, Lucy, and Linda Woolley. *Shoes.* London, England: V&A Publications, 1999.

Suede Buc

Bucs, or bucks, were rubber-soled shoes where the uppers were made of suede or buckskin, a pliable leather with a soft, brushed surface. They were styled after the classic oxford shoe, which laced over the instep, or the upper part of the foot that is curved and that lies between the ankle and toes. The soles of the shoes were either red rubber or blackened rubber. First popularized in the 1920s, white buckskin shoes were worn throughout the 1930s by the most fashionable men at vacation resorts and sporting events. Another popular color for Bucs was dirty Buc, so-named because the light tan color blended with dirt. In the days when men regularly polished their shoes, Bucs were an easy-care item. If they showed any discoloring from grime, all their owners had to do was quickly brush them. Bucs were marketed in the United States by G. H. Bass, a footwear manufacturer.

The popularity of the Buc may be directly linked to Great Britain's Prince of Wales, later Edward VIII (1894–1972). Edward wore suede shoes with sporty suits at a time when it was considered a fashion mistake to wear casual shoes with suits. He even initiated a controversy when he donned brown suede shoes with a dark blue suit, which was considered an inappropriate match. Combining the two was eventually accepted, however, because Edward was considered a fashion trendsetter.

During World War II (1939–45) Bucs went out of style because the leather and rubber required to produce them were needed for the war effort. When men exited the military at the end of the war, they longed to return to the comforts of civilian life. This yearning for informality resulted in more casual clothing styles and the renewed popularity of the Buc. The shoe was more comfortable than the traditional 1930s stiff leather business shoe, even though it basically was the same cut, or the rigid standard-issue low leather military boot or blucher that soldiers wore throughout the war. During the postwar years Bucs became fashionable casual shoes. While formality still ruled in the workplace, men occasionally wore Bucs in darker colors for business purposes with woolen worsted, a lightweight wool, or tweed suits.

For More Information

Pratt, Lucy, and Linda Woolley. *Shoes*. London, England: V&A Publications, 1999.

Schoeffler, O. E., and William Gale. *Esquire's Encyclopedia of 20th Century Men's Fashions*. New York: McGraw-Hill, 1973.

Weejuns

By the mid-1930s shoes handmade by Norwegian fishermen during their off-season became incredibly popular in Great Britain and the United States. These leather shoes featured slip-on styling, a moccasin toe, which was identified by the U-shaped leather inset stitched around the top of the shoe's front, and a strap sewn across the instep. The strap on Weejuns often had a diamond-shaped cutout in the center. These shoes came to be known as loafers in later decades. A variation on this moccasin-toe shoe was called the Norwegian-front shoe and featured laces over the instep. Weejuns were typically made in solid colors, but some styles were made of contrasting pieces of dark and light leather. These shoes became an important part of the fashionable preppy look of the 1950s and 1980s.

SEE ALSO *Volume 5, 1946–60: Preppy Look*

For More Information

Schoeffler, O. E., and William Gale. *Esquire's Encyclopedia of 20th Century Men's Fashions*. New York: McGraw-Hill, 1973.

Young, William H. and Nancy K. Young. *1930s*. Westport, CT: Greenwood Press, 2002.

Where to Learn More

The following list of resources focuses on material appropriate for middle school or high school students. Please note that the Web site addresses were verified prior to publication, but are subject to change.

Books

Batterberry, Michael, and Ariane Batterberry. *Fashion: The Mirror of History.* New York: Greenwich House, 1977.

Bigelow, Marybelle S. *Fashion in History: Apparel in the Western World.* Minneapolis, MN: Burgess Publishing, 1970.

Boucher, François. *20,000 Years of Fashion: The History of Costume and Personal Adornment.* Extended ed. New York: Harry N. Abrams, 1987.

Contini, Mila. *Fashion: From Ancient Egypt to the Present Day.* Edited by James Laver. New York: Odyssey Press, 1965.

Corson, Richard. *Fashions in Hair: The First Five Thousand Years.* London, England: Peter Owen, 2001.

Cosgrave, Bronwyn. *The Complete History of Costume and Fashion: From Ancient Egypt to the Present Day.* New York: Checkmark Books, 2000.

Ewing, Elizabeth; revised and updated by Alice Mackrell. *History of Twentieth Century Fashion.* Lanham, MD: Barnes and Noble Books, 1992.

Hoobler, Dorothy, and Thomas Hoobler. *Vanity Rules: A History of American Fashion and Beauty.* Brookfield, CT: Twenty-First Century Books, 2000.

Laver, James. *Costume and Fashion: A Concise History.* 4th ed. London, England: Thames and Hudson, 2002.

Lawlor, Laurie. *Where Will This Shoe Take You?: A Walk through the History of Footwear.* New York: Walker and Co., 1996.

Lister, Margot. *Costume: An Illustrated Survey from Ancient Times to the Twentieth Century.* London, England: Herbert Jenkins, 1967.

Miller, Brandon Marie. *Dressed for the Occasion: What Americans Wore 1620-1970.* Minneapolis, MN: Lerner Publications, 1999.

Mulvagh, Jane. *Vogue History of 20th Century Fashion.* New York: Viking, 1988.

Payne, Blanche, Geitel Winakor, and Jane Farrell-Beck. *The History of Costume.* 2nd ed. New York: HarperCollins, 1992.

Peacock, John. *The Chronicle of Western Fashion: From Ancient Times to the Present Day.* New York: Harry N. Abrams, 1991.

Perl, Lila. *From Top Hats to Baseball Caps, from Bustles to Blue Jeans: Why We Dress the Way We Do.* New York: Clarion Books, 1990.

Pratt, Lucy, and Linda Woolley. *Shoes.* London, England: V&A Publications, 1999.

Racinet, Auguste. *The Historical Encyclopedia of Costumes.* New York: Facts on File, 1988.

Ribeiro, Aileen. *The Gallery of Fashion.* Princeton, NJ: Princeton University Press, 2000.

Rowland-Warne, L. *Costume.* New York: Dorling Kindersley, 2000.

Schnurnberger, Lynn Edelman. *Let There Be Clothes: 40,000 Years of Fashion.* New York: Workman, 1991.

Schoeffler, O. E., and William Gale. *Esquire's Encyclopedia of 20th Century Men's Fashions.* New York: McGraw-Hill, 1973.

Sichel, Marion. *History of Men's Costume.* New York: Chelsea House, 1984.

Steele, Valerie. *Fifty Years of Fashion: New Look to Now.* New Haven, CT: Yale University Press, 1997.

Trasko, Mary. *Daring Do's: A History of Extraordinary Hair.* New York: Flammarion, 1994.

Yarwood, Doreen. *The Encyclopedia of World Costume.* New York: Charles Scribner's Sons, 1978.

Yarwood, Doreen. *Fashion in the Western World, 1500–1990.* New York: Drama Book Publishers, 1992.

Web Sites

Bender, A. *La Couturière Parisienne. http://marquise.de/index.html* (accessed on January 7, 2013).

Kathie Rothkop Hair Design. *Hair History. http://www.hairrific.com/hist.htm* (accessed on January 7, 2013).

Ladnier, Penny D. Dunlap. *The Costume Gallery. http://www.costumegallery.com* (accessed on January 7, 2013).

Maginnis, Tara. *The Costumer's Manifesto. http://www.costumes.org/* (accessed on January 7, 2013).

Metropolitan Museum of Art. *The Costume Institute. http://www.metmuseum. org/about-the-museum/museum-departments/curatorial-departments/the-costume-institute* (accessed on January 7, 2013).

Museum of Costume, Bath. http://www.museumofcostume.co.uk (accessed on January 7, 2013).

Sardo, Julie Zetterberg. *The Costume Page. http://www.costumepage.org/* (accessed on January 7, 2013).

Thomas, Pauline Weston, and Guy Thomas. *Fashion-Era. http://www.fashion-era.com/index.htm* (accessed on January 7, 2013).

Index

Italic type indicates volume number; **boldface** indicates main entries; (ill.) indicates illustrations.

U